# EVERY KIND OF SMOCKING

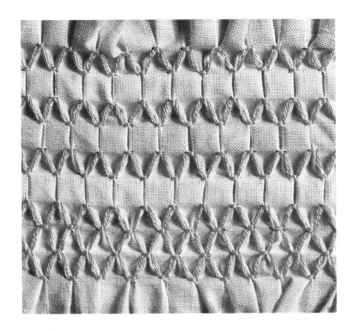

# EVERY KIND OF SMOCKING

### Edited by Kit Pyman
*Drawings by Jan Messent*

HENRY HOLT AND COMPANY
NEW YORK

First published in the United States in 1987 by
Henry Holt and Company, Inc., 521 Fifth Avenue,
New York, New York 10175

Distributed in Canada by Fitzhenry & Whiteside Limited
195 Allstate Parkway, Markham, Ontario L3R 4T8.

Library of Congress Catalog Card Number 86–82915
ISBN: 0-8050-0086-0
First American Edition

Typeset by Phoenix Photosetting, Chatham, England
Made and printed in Spain by Elkar S. Co-op, Bilbao 12

ISBN 0-8050-0086-0

# Contents

CHAPTER 1

# *Introduction.*
# *History of the smock*

# Introduction

In its simplest form, smocking is a decorative way of gathering a wide piece of fabric into a required measurement. It is one of the prettiest and easiest of needlework techniques.

Smocking, however, is more than this. It is also a method of manipulation, of changing the texture, the color, the weight and the flexibility of a fabric; and it is these qualities which make it such an interesting and adaptable technique.

Throughout this book, all kinds of smocking are explained and illustrated. Patterns are given for many of the designs, and other work is shown which offers different ideas for the use of smocking.

The book starts with the history of the smock: the development of the traditional pattern, the smocking stitches, the embroidery in the 'boxes' and the hand-made buttons.

The 'step by step' section next explains the basic technique of smocking, while three samplers – described in detail with explanatory diagrams – show how stitches can be combined in attractive patterns, and how designs can be built up.

A detailed pattern is given for a simple short smock which can be adapted to many different fabrics.

Children's clothes use smocking in a practical way to allow for growth and activity, and the fabrics are very suitable for gathering. Patterns are given for a variety of clothes for the early years of childhood, some with touches of embroidery which add to their small-scale charm.

Fashion has always varied with the climate of the times, although the simple shift reappears regularly and the short smock is perennially useful and attractive. Indeed, you may well be surprised at the number of ways in which smocking can be used today and this section provides many fascinating drawings and ideas. You will notice in each case that the smocking is an intrinsic part of the design, essential to the whole, giving no feeling that it has just been added as a decoration.

Smocking is also shown combined with other techniques such as beading, embroidery, appliqué and patchwork. Instructions and examples are also given for another kind of smocking which is sometimes called 'North American'; this technique is worked directly onto the marked fabric, gathering the surface into folded patterns, several of which are described and illustrated.

Experiments with smocking can lead to some interesting results, and some of them raise the technique from the realm of craft into that of art. Those who see stitchery more as a medium for expression than as a practical technique will be inspired by the ideas in the experimental smocking section.

Finally, a piece of smocking can be greatly enhanced by a careful choice of fastenings and finishes: a vest may be lightly held with fabric toggles, or a neckline tied with satin rouleaux; cuffs may be fastened with hand-made buttons in matching silk, or the edge of a collar emphasized with a line of colored stitchery. This last section of the book provides information on how to make rouleaux and piping, needle-made edgings and hand-made buttons.

Once you have learned the basic technique of smocking, I hope that the beautiful work illustrated in this book will encourage you to add your own contribution to the continuing tradition of smocking as both art and craft, which is such a great source of delight and inspiration.

# History of the smock

The rural smock in Britain, as we recognise it today, was in general use between 1770 and 1870. Originally a plain shirt-like garment, it developed fullness at the back and front to allow for ease of movement. The gathers were held in place with neat uniform stitches – the embroidery technique called smocking.

The basic garment takes many regional forms but the smocks fall roughly into two categories. The first is the coat smock which buttoned down the center front, and the second is the Round smock which had a small slit opening for the head and was reversible. The pockets were placed exactly at the side seam to allow the garment to be worn back to front; they were either real pockets with a flap, or just slits to allow the hand to reach the trouser pocket.

In essence, the smock was very simply cut from squares and rectangles, which was achieved economically by folding the fabric. The width of the available fabric was usually 36in. (92cm) and the amount required was three times the length from neck to hem. The fabric was then folded in three equal lengths – two lengths formed the front and the back of the

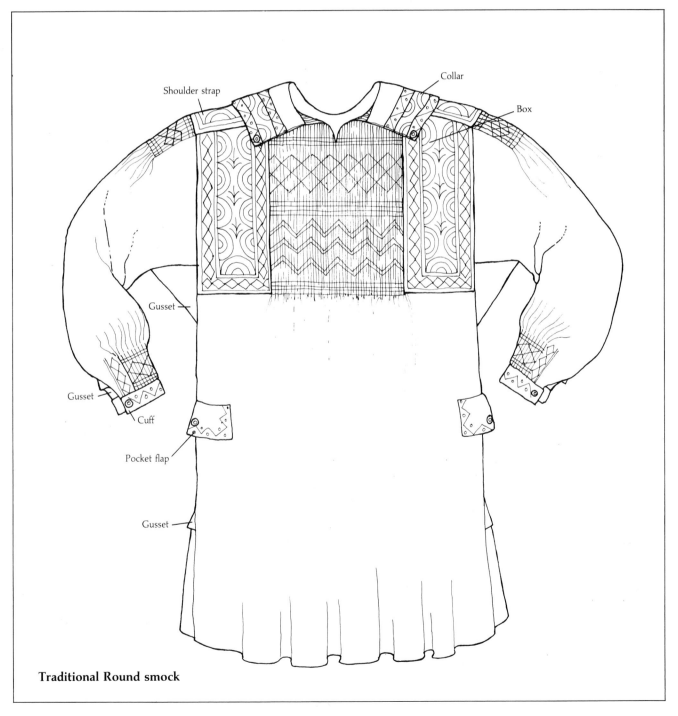

**Traditional Round smock**

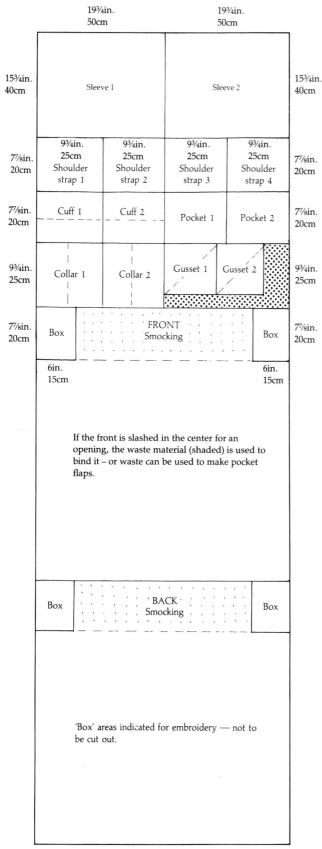

19¾in.
50cm

19¾in.
50cm

15¾in.
40cm

Sleeve 1

Sleeve 2

15¾in.
40cm

7⅞in.
20cm

9¾in.
25cm
Shoulder
strap 1

9¾in.
25cm
Shoulder
strap 2

9¾in.
25cm
Shoulder
strap 3

9¾in.
25cm
Shoulder
strap 4

7⅞in.
20cm

7⅞in.
20cm

Cuff 1

Cuff 2

Pocket 1

Pocket 2

7⅞in.
20cm

9¾in.
25cm

Collar 1

Collar 2

Gusset 1

Gusset 2

9¾in.
25cm

7⅞in.
20cm

Box

FRONT
Smocking

Box

7⅞in.
20cm

6in.
15cm

6in.
15cm

If the front is slashed in the center for an
opening, the waste material (shaded) is used to
bind it – or waste can be used to make pocket
flaps.

Box

BACK
Smocking

Box

'Box' areas indicated for embroidery — not to
be cut out.

**Traditional smock pattern.** *The length is three times the
measurement from neck to hem, folded into three equal sections. Two
of these sections form the front and back of the smock, and the third is
sub-divided for the sleeves, cuffs and collar, shoulder straps, pockets
and gussets. This pattern is based on fabric 39½in. (100cm) wide and
115½in. (315cm) long. Supplied by Clare Emery.*

smock, and the remaining third made the sleeves and cuffs,
the collar, gussets, shoulder straps and pockets.

The colors of smocks varied with the county of origin, and
ranged from white (which was popular for wedding smocks)
to natural unbleached, and green, blue and black.

The fabric was homespun linen, drabbette or cotton twill
which, being made of hemp or flax, was naturally very dura-
ble. The thread used for the embroidery was a hard twisted
linen. The buttons were of horn, bone, metal or glass.

Earlier eighteenth-century smocks are generally quite plain,
having a little smocking to hold in the fullness. The elabo-
rately embroidered smocks, with the embroidered 'boxes' on
either side of the smocking, are usually nineteenth-century in
origin. It has generally been supposed previously that the
symbols in the boxes denoted the trade of the wearer; but the
view today is that the designs are of natural origin, as the spir-
als, trees and flower forms are found in most country crafts.

The embroidery stitches found in the boxes, on the cuffs
and on the shoulder straps are very simple and consist of
variations on Feather, Chain and Stem stitch. On the 'tubing',
or gathers, the smocking stitches are Stem, Cable and Trellis.
Tension and regular working were the most important factors
rather than elaborate patterning. The smocking held in the
fullness, and the other embroidery was also functional in that
it protected the fabric from wear and strengthened weak areas
such as the shoulders and cuffs.

The making of a smock was often a home occupation, starting with the spinning and weaving of the cloth. Mothers,
daughters and girl-friends would make up smocks for their
menfolk. In some areas the making of smocks was a cottage
industry. The ready-cut garment, block printed with the
embroidery design, was collected from the factory, smocked
and embroidered by the villagers, and then returned to the
factory where it was assembled and distributed to shops and
markets. Smocks were expensive to buy, the price in 1796
being the equivalent of two weeks wages for a working man.

Essentially an overall, the smock was worn by shepherds
and agricultural laborers, waggoners and carters, drovers and
woodmen. It protected clothing from dirt and dust, and wear
and tear. The demise of the smock came about with the inven-
tion and development of farm machinery, because the volu-
minous folds were likely to be caught in the fast-moving
mechanisms.

As so often happens when a utility garment is abandoned
by the working classes, it becomes adopted by the fashionable. Men of the nineteenth century involved with William
Morris and the Pre-Raphaelite movement wore the garment
as an artists' smock, and women adapted it as aesthetic dress.
Smocking was also seen on Liberty print dresses, silk
teagowns, blouses and baby clothes. Patterns and instructions appeared in ladies' magazines and smocked garments
could be purchased in all the fashionable shops.

Opposite above
**Sampler of traditional smocking stitches.** *Worked on natural
linen. By Gail Marsh.*

Opposite below
**Sampler of traditional embroidery for smocks, with
handmade buttons.** *By Gail Marsh.*

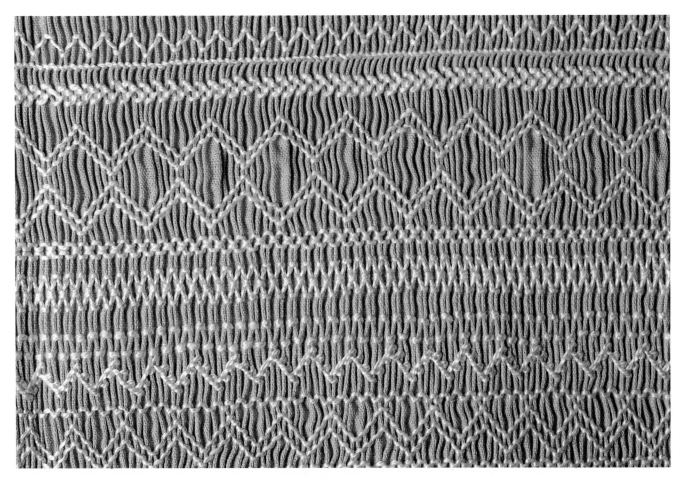

Recently the smock has become a fashion garment, and interest has revived in the construction of the traditional smock as a wearable garment for any age group.

Smocking is a most versatile technique, and the availability of interesting fabrics has opened up new possibilities. Smocked garments can be as different as a thick winter coat, a delicate blouse, a baby's romper suit or a high-fashion evening dress. Smocking is also being used in a variety of ways – for accessories, furnishings, and even dramatic wall hangings; examples of these are also illustrated in the following pages.

**Traditional Round smock.** *By Sheila Sturrock. Cut from a 'thirds' pattern in calico, and embroidered with embroidery floss.*

# CHAPTER 2

# *Smocking step-by-step*

# Smocking step-by-step

## CHOOSING THE FABRIC

The most practical fabrics for smocking are of light to medium weight; they should be evenly woven and have a smooth surface. Suitable choices for general use are cotton poplin, calicoes, lightweight denim, cotton lawn, plain and printed polyester/cotton blends, silk, satin, organdy, and light wool mixtures.

Fabrics to be avoided until experience has been gained are pile fabrics, such as velvet and corduroy, stretch materials, and knits of all kinds. Once the basic technique has been mastered, however, these fabrics are interesting to use.

For a first piece of work choose a plain fabric in a pastel color, which is easy on the eye when counting the dots.

## CHOOSING THE COLORED THREADS

Keep the color scheme simple, i.e., the shades and tones should be of not more than three or four colors.

A whole skein looks much brighter than a single thread, so test the thread against the fabric by pulling out a length. By the time the strands are split and the smocking stretches, the actual stitches can 'disappear' altogether if the color scheme is too subtle.

Choose a contrast in tone as well as in color. Half-shut your eyes and look at the threads – there should be clear steps of light, medium and dark tones. Your smocking will be viewed from a distance, and if the colors are too close in tone the rows will merge together.

Think of fresh, clean colors for children (as in Sampler 1, page 18), and more sophisticated colors for adults. When working on a print make sure that the thread is a strong contrast, but relates to a color already there.

Six-strand embroidery floss can be used for smocking. Experiment with the number of strands – four strands often gives a richer effect than three as the embroidery stretches when the gathering threads are removed and the stitches move further apart. Other threads, such as coton à broder and pearl cotton, come in different thicknesses and look very attractive as they have a high sheen.

## PREPARATION OF FABRIC

Smocking is always worked on the grain of the fabric, preferably from selvage to selvage. The top and bottom of the piece can be straightened by tearing or cutting along the weft thread.

It is wise to pre-shrink fabrics before starting a project. To do this, neaten the raw edges to prevent fraying and wash as you would the finished garment. Dry, and iron smooth.

## AMOUNT OF FABRIC REQUIRED

As a general rule, the width of the fabric should be three times the width of the finished smocking – approximately 3in. (8cm) of fabric will result in 1in. (2.5cm) of smocking. However this varies slightly according to the spacing of the dots and the tension of the stitches; it is advisable therefore to work a small sampler to calculate the exact measurements before starting work.

The smocking should be completed before the garment is sewn together. Since many smocking patterns require double yokes and cuffs, and other areas which enclose the raw edges, check on this in case extra fabric is required.

## GRIDS FOR GATHERING THE FABRIC

Smocking consists of embroidery stitches worked on tubes of fabric, which have been formed by regular lines of gathering of rows of exactly spaced stitches. The basis of this grid can be a transfer, pencil dots, counted threads or the printed pattern of the fabric, such as polka dots or checks.

## SMOCKING DOT TRANSFERS

Dot transfers are available in a wide range of sizes, and the gauge should be chosen with the fabric and the finished effect in mind. Closely spaced dots are suitable for fine fabrics and give small shallow tubes; widely spaced dots result in deep pleats and are more suitable for heavier fabrics. As a rough guide, dots that are $\frac{2}{10}$in. (5mm) to $\frac{3}{10}$in. (7.5mm) apart are suitable for blouse-weight cotton polyester or cotton lawn.

Cut out the fabric on the grain, and press it smooth. The dots are applied to the wrong side of the fabric. Cut the manufacturer's name from the transfer and test this on a small piece of fabric for iron temperature (be careful that the iron is not too hot for a fabric with synthetic fibers). The test piece can also be used to check if the transfer will wash out.

Lay the fabric on the ironing board, wrong side uppermost. Cut the sheet of smocking dots to the correct size, allowing an extra row of dots top and bottom – these auxiliary rows will keep the dots even when you work the embroidery – and lay the sheet wax side down on the fabric. Pin it in position – the dots should be in line with the grain of the fabric. Set the iron to the correct temperature. Do not slide the iron back and forth as the dots will smudge, but press each area for approximately ten seconds. Lift a corner of the paper to make sure that all the dots have transferred properly before you peel off the transfer.

## OTHER METHODS OF MARKING THE DOTS

### Graph paper

Place the prepared fabric on a hard smooth surface, wrong side uppermost. Place a sheet of dressmaker's carbon paper on top, colored side down. Pin a sheet of graph paper in position over this. With a hard, sharp pencil point make a dot at each measured intersection. (Used transfer papers can be employed instead of graph paper.)

### Templates

Draw a grid on thick paper or thin card, and make a hole with a stiletto or a sharp thick needle at each intersection. Place the template in position over the wrong side of the fabric and mark dots through each hole. This is a useful method as the template can be used again and again.

### Tissue paper

This method is useful when the chosen fabric is so fine and transparent that marked dots might remain visible. Plot the dot pattern onto tissue paper and baste this in position on the wrong side of the fabric. Gather directly through the tissue and the fabric, and when the gathering is completed gently tear the tissue paper away.

### Pleating or smock-gathering machine

Machines are available in different widths that stitch up to 32 rows of gathers simultaneously. They are extremely efficient and take much of the preliminary labor out of smocking; but they are only really suitable for the lighter-weight fabrics.

### POSITIONING THE ROWS OF DOTS

Most smocking is worked on the straight of the grain of the fabric. Leave a good allowance for seams, and mark an extra row of dots at the top and bottom to stabilize the pleating and ease the insertion of the gathered fabric into the rest of the garment. If a slight curve is required, then the lines of gathers can be graded to accommodate it, but a full curve inserted in a curved yoke requires a widening of the dot pattern.

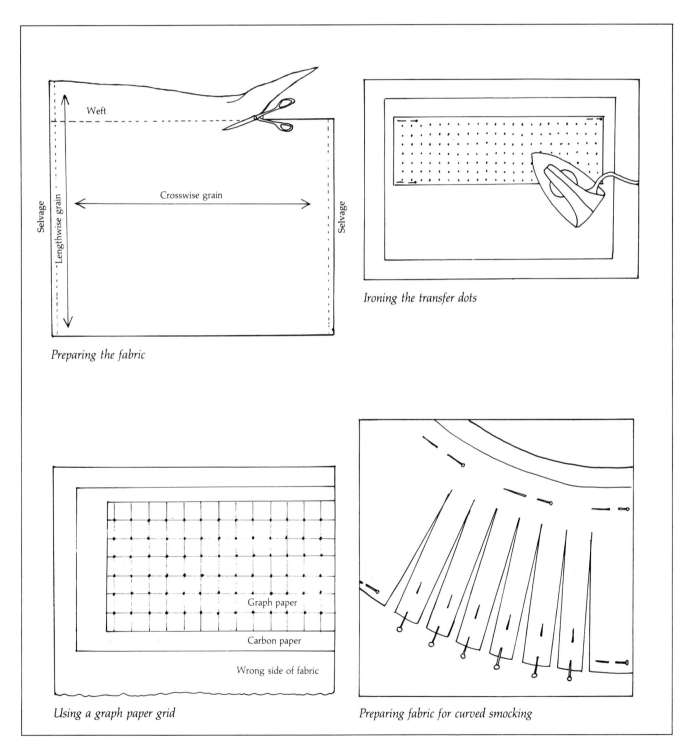

*Preparing the fabric*

*Ironing the transfer dots*

*Using a graph paper grid*

*Preparing fabric for curved smocking*

## Curved shapes

This can be achieved by slashing the transfer sheet up to the second row of dots and spreading the paper into the correct curve, keeping the spacing as even as possible. Pin the transfer paper in position and proceed as already described.

## Pointed shapes

Points look particularly attractive on children's clothes, sleeve heads and skirts. Any of the methods of transfering dots can be used, but make sure there is an even number of dots at the point, such as two or four. Increase the width of the triangle by one dot on each side until the point is the required length, and then gather as for straight smocking.

## Dots over seams

It is more convenient to put the dots on the fabric while the fabric is flat, and before sewing up the seams. However, to make sure that the fabric is evenly gathered, the vertical row of dots should fall on the seamline on both pieces – a small adjustment may be made in the seam allowance to accommodate this. Sew the seam exactly through the middle of the dots. When the fabric is gathered, the seam dot is treated as one dot, and the seam then falls between the tubes on the right side and does not interfere with the embroidery.

## Threads, needles and other equipment

The thread used for gathering needs to be strong in proportion to the weight of the fabric. Mercerized cotton or polyester-wrapped cotton thread can be used for light to medium fabrics, and buttonhole twist for heavy fabrics. A light coating of beeswax stops thread from snarling. Use a contrasting colored thread for gathering – this acts as a guide to keeping the embroidery neat and straight.

Use the kind of needle called 'sharps' for gathering, and a crewel needle with a long eye for the embroidery. Choose a size that will pass easily through the fabric with its accompanying thread – if there is any difficulty in pulling it through then the needle is too small.

Small, sharp embroidery scissors are needed for cutting threads, and a thimble (if you use one). Pins should be fine enough not to mark the fabric. The usual dressmaking equipment will be required for the cutting out and assembly of the garments.

## Gathering

Cut out the required fabric with a good seam allowance. If the fabric is likely to fray, overlock or hand-whip the raw edges. Cut the gathering thread longer than the width of the fabric, and make a knot in one end. Start at the right side if you are right-handed, and at the left if you are left-handed. Take a small stitch picking up the first dot. If the fabric is loosely woven take another stitch over this to secure it. Continue across the row picking up a tiny amount of fabric at each dot: this need not be done individually as the fabric can be slid on to the needle and a dozen stitches can be taken at a time. At the end of the row, leave the thread hanging. Work all the rows, including the extra ones at the top and bottom.

Pull up the gathering threads to the required width, which should be slightly narrower than the finished width (here a previously worked sampler will prove invaluable). Tie off the threads securely in pairs, making sure that the width is consistent down the length of the fabric. The tubes should lie uniformly side by side, but not so tightly that a needle cannot be inserted between them.

Pull the gathers lengthways to set the tubes in position. Turn the fabric to the right side and look at the gathers. Think of them as 'tubes' and 'valleys'; the tubes are deeper on the right side to allow for the embroidery. It is at this stage that the center valley should be marked with a contrasting colored thread, by counting the tubes. This is for symmetrical designs that are centered, for example, on the front of a yoke.

## General rules for smocking

Start the embroidery with a knot, coming up the side of the first tube to the right side of the fabric. To make a figure-of-eight knot, hold the end of the thread in the left hand, take the threaded end of the needle down and around the end (a), and then back up and through the top loop from front to back as in (b). Pull tight and trim the free end.

Work from left to right if you are right-handed, and vice versa if left-handed. The needle is always horizontal, and it is the throwing of the thread that governs the position of the stitch. As a general rule when travelling up, throw the thread to the bottom, and when travelling down throw the thread to the top.

Fasten off the thread at the back of the last tube with a knot (see diagram above). Never stitch two tubes together when fastening off because they will then be held together when the gathers are removed and will destroy the effect.

The gathering threads are the guides to keep the smocking regular, straight and even. When you work between gathering threads keep in mind quarter, half and three-quarter steps to the next gathering thread, and your stitches will be neat.

Larger-scale motifs or patterns can be started in the center. In a large diamond design, for example, the point of the diamond will stitch together the two tubes on either side of the marked center valley. Start from this point and work out to one side. Reverse the smocking and work out from the same point to the other side. When the first row has been placed, then it is often possible to continue the pattern sequence from the side as usual.

The stitch should lie like a bead around a tube – if it is too tight then the embroidery will look skimpy; if it is too loose then the finished work will stretch like elastic. Practice on a sampler to achieve a good tension.

## Finishing

When the smocking is completed, remove the gathering threads by snipping the knotted ends. The smocking will stretch slightly and the appearance is much improved by steaming or 'setting'.

## Setting the gathers

Place the smocking right side down on the ironing board and pin to the correct width. Hold a steam iron above the fabric and allow the steam to set the gathers. Do not allow the iron to touch the smocking, or the tubes will be flattened. If a steam iron is not available, then use a damp cloth and the heat from a dry iron.

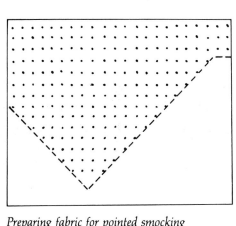

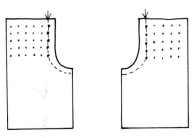

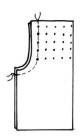

*Vertical row of dots on seam line*

*Seam-stitched through dots*

*Preparing fabric for pointed smocking*

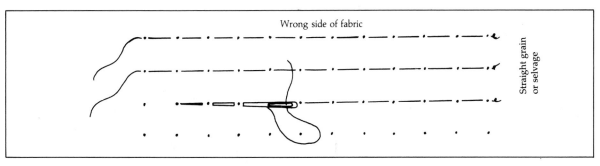

*Gathering from right to left*

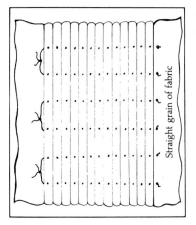

*Gathering-threads pulled up and tied in pairs*

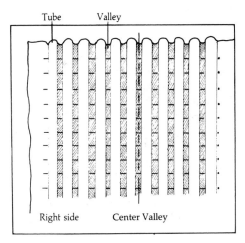

*Marking the center valley*

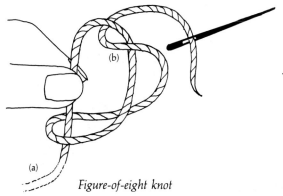

*Figure-of-eight knot*

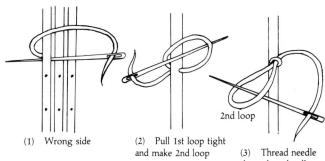

(1) Wrong side

(2) Pull 1st loop tight and make 2nd loop

(3) Thread needle through and pull tight. Trim end

*Fastening-off knot*

# Working a Sampler

Working a sampler is a good way of learning the stitches and understanding the need for an even tension; it is also an opportunity for trying out attractive color schemes and will remain a valuable reference for future projects.

All the samplers are worked on a piece of cotton or polycotton approximately 24in. (60cm) wide by 12in. (30cm) deep. Transfer the required numbers and rows of dots to the wrong side, gather with contrasting thread and pull up.

Four strands of embroidery floss are used throughout. Leave the first row of gathering (marked 'auxiliary row') which is to keep the gathers even, and start on the next row as Line 1. 'Lines' refer to lines of gathering, and 'Rows' refer to rows of smocking stitches. Always work the stitches from left to right (or vice versa if you are left-handed) unless specifically instructed not to do so.

# Sampler 1

All the stitches on this sampler are related to one another.

Mark or transfer 17 rows of at least 60 dots (transfer sheet ²⁄₁₀in. × ³⁄₁₀in. or 5mm × 7.5mm) gather with contrast thread, pull up, and tie.

Select four colors of six-strand embroidery floss, and work with four strands at a time. Leave the first row of gathering (marked 'auxiliary row'), which is to keep the gathers even, and start on the next row as Line 1.

ROW 1. *Stem stitch* – also known as Rope and Outline stitch

Bring the needle up on the left of tube 1. Throw thread to the bottom and pick up tube 2. Throw thread to the bottom and pick up tube 3, and continue across the row. The needle should be horizontal and parallel to the gathering thread; the stitch should be 1mm deep for fine fabric. Finish by taking the needle down to the right of the last tube, and knot off.

*Mock Chain stitch*

Work another row of Stem stitch directly below the first, this time throwing the thread to the top before each stitch. This forms a chain effect.

ROW 2. *Cable stitch*

Bring the needle up on the left of tube 1. Throw the thread to the bottom and pick up tube 2. Throw the thread to the top and pick up tube 3. Continue across the row alternately throwing the thread to the top and bottom. This procedure is referred to as 'cable up' and 'cable down' when combined with the following stitches.

Stem, Cable and Mock Chain are all tight stitches and are often used as the first row of smocking to set the gathers evenly. They are especially useful at the neck edge of a yoke where the gathers are closer together. (Zigzag Cable will be found in Row 1 of the second sampler).

ROWS 3 and 4. *Diamond stitch*

Bring the needle up on the left of tube 1. Cable up and pick up tube 2. Throw thread to top and pick up tube 3 half-way between the rows of gathers. Cable down and pick up tube 4. Throw thread to the bottom and pick up tube 5 level with row

3 gathering. Cable up and pick up tube 6. Continue along the row. The second row completing the diamond can be started on row 4, coming up to meet the stitches of the first row. Alternatively, you can come back along the row by reversing the work and holding it upside down.

ROWS 5, 6 and 7. *Wave stitch*

Bring the needle up on the left of tube 1 on row 6. Cable down and pick up tube 2. With your eye, divide the space between rows 6 and 5 into quarter, half and three-quarter steps – throw the thread to the bottom and pick up tube 3 at the quarter step. Throw the thread to the bottom and pick up tube 4 at the half step. Throw the thread to the bottom and pick up tube 5 at the three-quarter step. Throw the thread to the bottom and pick up tube 6 level with row 5 gathering. Cable up and pick up tube 7. Come down in the same steps, throwing the thread to the top, and cable down on tube 12.

There should be four stitches between the top and bottom cables, although any number of steps can be taken as long as they are even and consistent. The next two rows of Wave stitch are worked half a row below one another. (Trellis stitch which is similar is found in Sampler 3.)

ROW 5. *Small Cable flowerettes*

The flowerettes should be centered to match the points of the Wave stitch, and consist of four stitches. Stitch 1: – bring the needle up on the left of tube A and cable down and pick up tube B. Stitch 2: – cable up and pick up tube C. Stitch 3: – cable up and pick up tube D. Stitch 4: – put needle back down between tubes A and B. Knot off at the back.

When working individual motifs, the thread must be started and finished at the back without tying the tubes together. Do not try and jump from one motif to another because the smocking will not expand when the gathers are removed.

ROWS 8 and 9. *Links*

This is a combination of cables and diamonds. Bring the needle up on the left side of tube 1, half-way between rows 8 and 9. Follow the diagram carefully, counting the number of cable stitches before working the Diamond stitch down again. Complete by working a second row directly beneath.

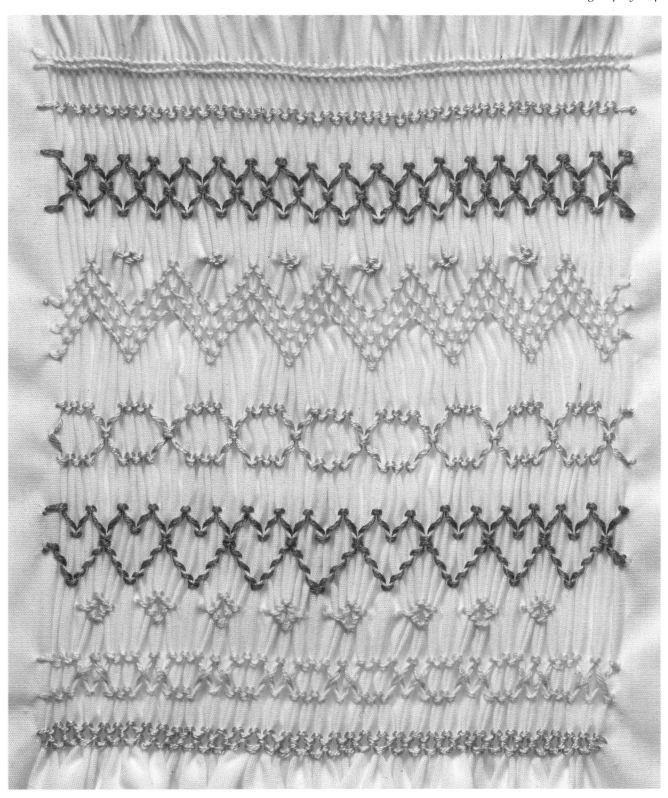

**ROWS 10, 11 and 12.** *Hearts*

The hearts are a combination of Diamond stitch and Wave stitch. Work a row of Diamond stitch coming half-way down between rows of gatherings. Work Wave stitch, as shown in the diagram, to complete the hearts. This is a three-step wave, so divide the space into thirds to keep the stitches even.

**Sampler 1.** *By Gail Marsh.*

**ROW BETWEEN 12 and 13.** *Large Cable flowerettes*

Each flowerette consists of eight stitches. Follow the instructions as for the small flowerette, noting the order of stitches. Knot off after each motif is worked.

*Every kind of smocking*

ROWS 14 and 15. *Crossed diamonds*

Follow the diagram and work five Cable stitches on row 14, then a Diamond stitch down to row 15, then back up to row 14 and Cable again. The second row starts on row 15 and the Diamond stitch goes up to row 14 above, thus crossing the

threads. This is particularly effective when worked in two colors.

ROW 16. *Double Cable*

Work a row of Cable stitch, and then work a second row immediately beneath. Match the stitches carefully as shown in the diagram.

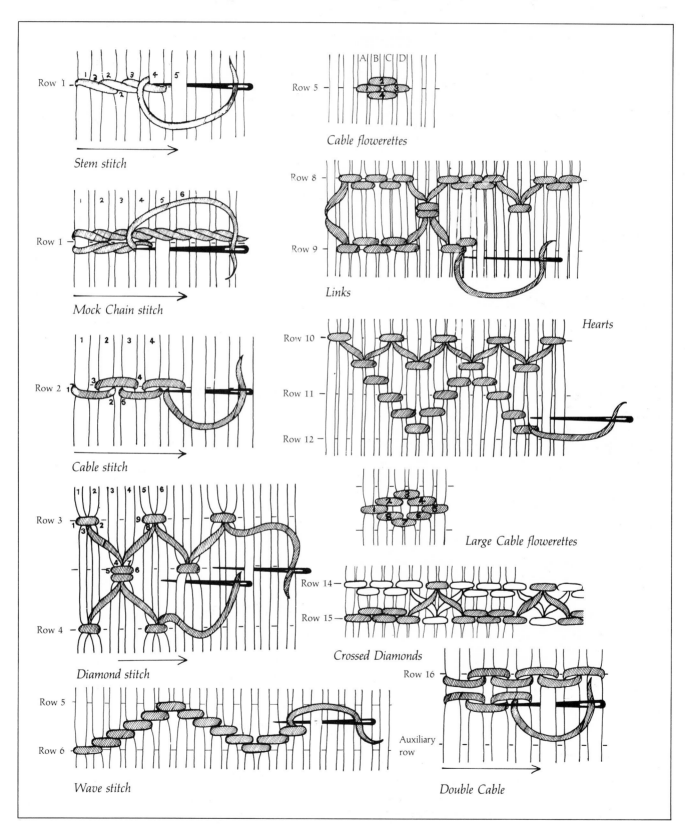

Stem stitch

Mock Chain stitch

Cable stitch

Diamond stitch

Wave stitch

Cable flowerettes

Links

Hearts

Large Cable flowerettes

Crossed Diamonds

Double Cable

20

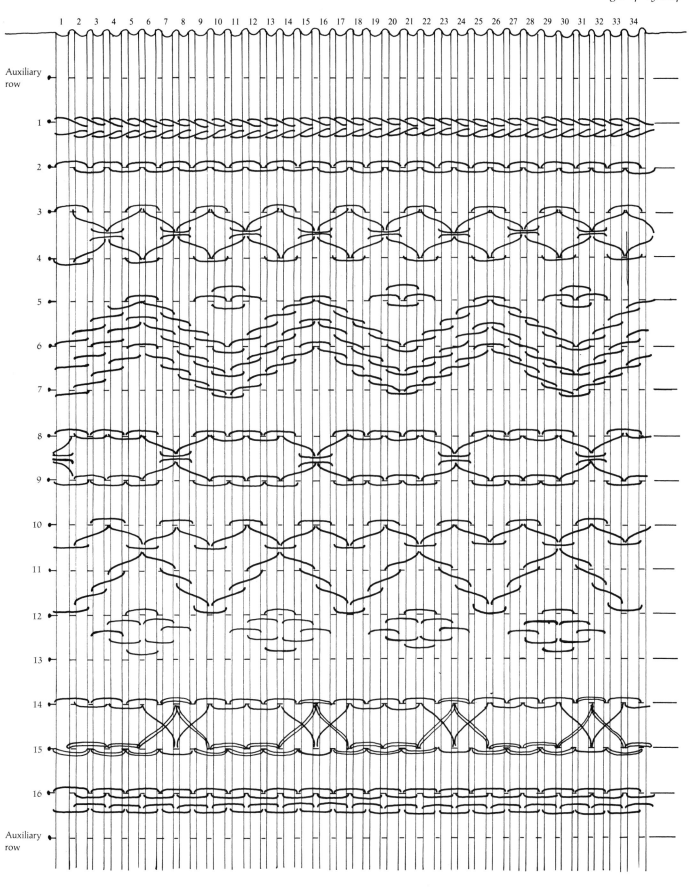

**Diagram of Sampler 1.** *By Gail Marsh. Smocking instructions are often set in a diagrammatic form. When you are familiar with the* *stitches it is easy to follow the symbols.*

# Sampler 2

This sampler has a greater variety of stitches, many of them borrowed from other embroidery techniques. Note that, with these new stitches, *two* tubes are picked up together.

Mark or tranfer 12 rows of at least 60 dots (transfer sheet ²⁄₁₀in. × ³⁄₁₀in., or 5mm × 7.5mm). Gather with contrast thread, pull up, and tie. The color scheme is two shades of the fabric color combined with white, worked with four strands in the needle. Leave the first row of gathering, and start on the next row as Line 1.

## ROW 1. *Zigzag Cable*

Work a row of Cable stitch, as in row 2 of Sampler 1 (page 18), along the gathering line. This stitch is often used as a first row to set the gathers. Then begin again on the left of tube 1 at A (in the diagram below). Cable down and pick up tube 2, cable up and pick up tube 3, take needle down to the back of the work between tubes 4 and 5 at B. Come back up between tubes 4 and 5 below the first row of cable at C. Follow the diagram to produce the Zigzag Cable stitch.

## ROWS 2–4 left. *Honeycomb stitch*

A block of Honeycomb stitch is worked on the left half of the sampler, and a block of Surface Honeycomb on the right half, illustrating the different effects of these two stitches.

Bring the needle up on the left of tube 1. Throw thread to the top and pick up tubes 2 and 1, and come out at A (see the Honeycomb stitch diagram). Take needle back to B and insert down the back of the tube to C. Throw thread to the bottom

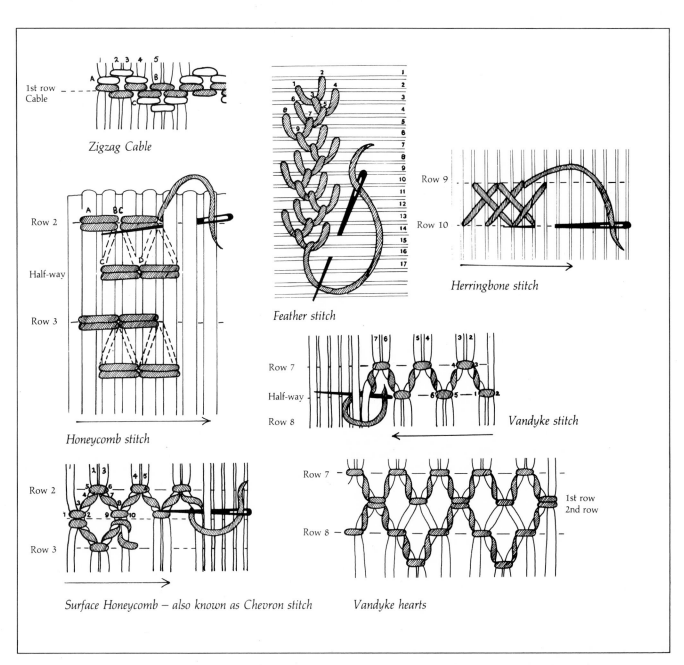

*Zigzag Cable*

*Honeycomb stitch*

*Surface Honeycomb – also known as Chevron stitch*

*Feather stitch*

*Herringbone stitch*

*Vandyke stitch*

*Vandyke hearts*

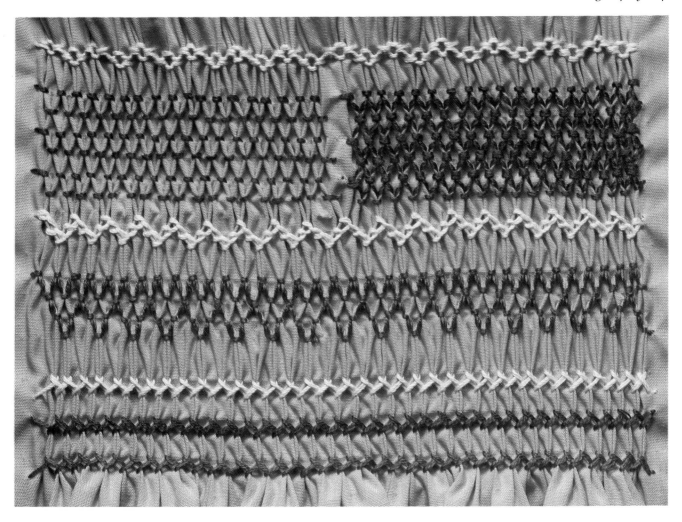

and pick up tubes 3 and 4, coming out at C. Take needle across to D and insert up the back of the tube coming out at E. Repeat across the row. The second row of Honeycomb stitch starts on the row below.

*Honeycomb stitch* is very elastic and needs only 2 times or 2½ times the finished width of material.

ROWS 2–4 right. *Surface Honeycomb – also known as Chevron stitch*

This stitch has the same elasticity as Honeycomb stitch. Bring the needle out on the left of tube 1 half-way between the gathering lines. Throw the thread to the bottom and pick up tube 2. Throw the thread to the bottom and pick up tube 2 again level with the top row of gathering. Throw the thread to the top and pick up tube 3. Throw the thread to the top and pick up tube 3 again, half-way down. Repeat across the row. The second row of Surface Honeycomb is begun at the same point as the first and the diamond shape is completed.

ROW 5. *Feather stitch*

Feather stitch is easier to work if you turn the fabric and work towards yourself. Pick up two tubes with each stitch. Keep the line straight by working between two rows of gathers.

**Sampler 2.** *By Gail Marsh.*

ROWS 6½ to 8. *Vandyke stitch*

Vandyke stitch is the only stitch worked from right to left (and vice versa for left-handers). Vandyke stitch is very elastic. Counting the tubes from the right, bring the needle up on the left of tube 2. Throw the thread to the bottom and pick up tubes 1 and 2 together. Throw the thread to the bottom and pick up tubes 2 and 3, half a space above. Throw the thread to the top and pick up tubes 2 and 3 again. Throw the thread to the top and come down and pick up tubes 3 and 4. Throw the thread to the bottom and pick up tubes 3 and 4 again. Repeat across the row.

*Vandyke hearts*

Under the first row of Vandyke stitch work a second row. Make each alternate stitch step down half a space to form the 'hearts'.

ROWS 9–11. *Herringbone stitch*

This is another stitch borrowed from embroidery which is often used with smocking. Pick two tubes up with each stitch. Do not make the stitch too wide since it is very elastic.

The last row of Herringbone stitch is repeated, to keep the tubes straight in pairs between the lines of embroidery.

# Sampler 3

The third sampler shows how Cable stitch may be used to make a basket motif. Embroidery stitches, such as Chain and French knots, can be used to create the tiny flowers. Mark the center valley so that the design is symmetrical, and start the Trellis stitch in the center and work out to the sides.

Mark or transfer 16 rows of 110 dots (transfer sheet $^{2}/_{10}$in. × $^{3}/_{10}$in. or 5mm × 7.5mm). Gather with contrast thread, pull up, and tie.

The colors are pale green, yellow, blue, and dark pink, and all the stitchery is done with four strands in the needle, although embroidery stitches such as French knots may require only three strands.

ROW 1. *Stem stitch.* (Page 18)

ROW 2. *Cable stitch.* (Page 18)

ROW 3. *Stem stitch.* (Page 18)

13 ROWS (approximately) of *Trellis stitch.* Start in the center and work a row of Wave stitch (page 18) and then work a second row underneath to complete a diamond.

## CENTER MOTIF

Work as shown on the diagram (page 26). Start the basket at the stitch, marked $x$, which lies over the center valley on line 9, and work out evenly to both sides. Once the top line of the basket has been determined you can work down to the base, reversing the work to come back along alternate rows. Work the handle last, remembering to reverse the direction of the stitch at the center valley. The blue outline is started at the center bottom of the basket and worked up both sides, leaving enough thread to tie in a bow at the top of the handle. Secure the bow with a stitch from the back. Baskets can be made any size according to the space available.

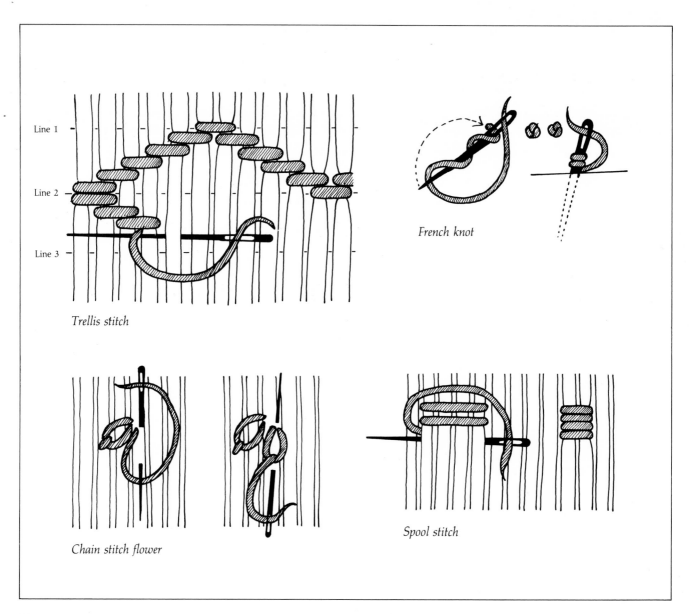

Line 1

Line 2

Line 3

*Trellis stitch*

*French knot*

*Chain stitch flower*

*Spool stitch*

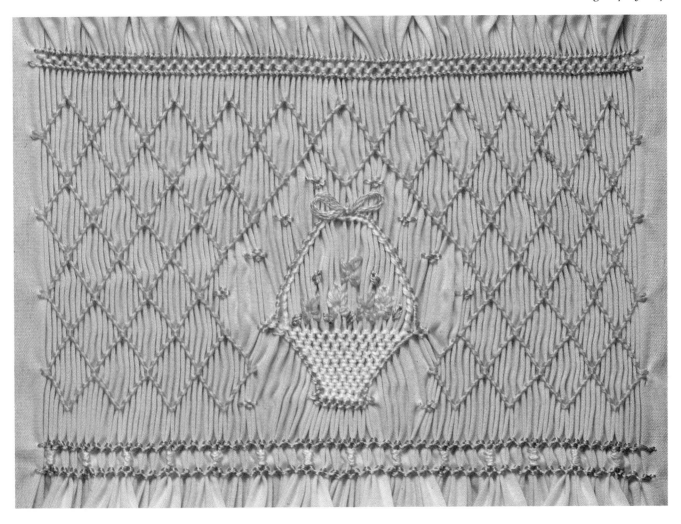

**Flowers**

The petals are in detached Chain stitch worked either down a tube or across two or three tubes. The centers could be French knots, or Bullion knots which are bolder.

The tiny blue flowers around the basket are small cable flowerettes, as on page 18.

ROW 14. *Cable stitch*

**Sampler 3.** *By Gail Marsh.*

Between ROWS 14 and 15. *Spool stitch*. As well as being used between these two rows of Cable stitch, Spool stitch is also used for the part of the basket handle that is vertical. Spool stitch can be used over any number of tubes, but, remember, it will prevent the smocking from being so elastic.

ROW 15. *Cable stitch*

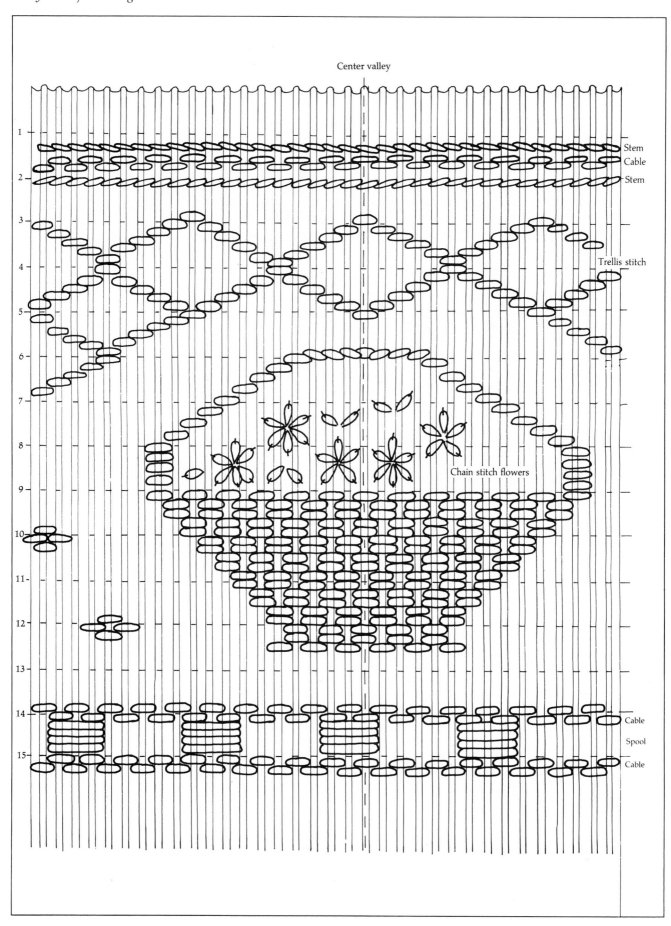

**Diagram of center of Sampler 3.** *By Gail Marsh.*

# Using striped, dotted and check fabrics

All these fabrics may be gathered without any dot preparation if the print or weave is accurate. Gather, as usual, on the wrong side of the fabric.

## STRIPED FABRICS

Narrow stripes: pick up each stripe at equal distances apart. Wide stripes: pick up the middle of each stripe at equal distances apart.

## Dots

Pick up the dots on alternate rows so that the tubes are straight. Check that the print is reasonably accurate and does not run off or out of line.

## Checks and ginghams

Woven checks and ginghams are always accurate, but be careful of printed checks. Make the gathers even on the grid, and the distance between the stitches and the rows compatible with the size of the check.

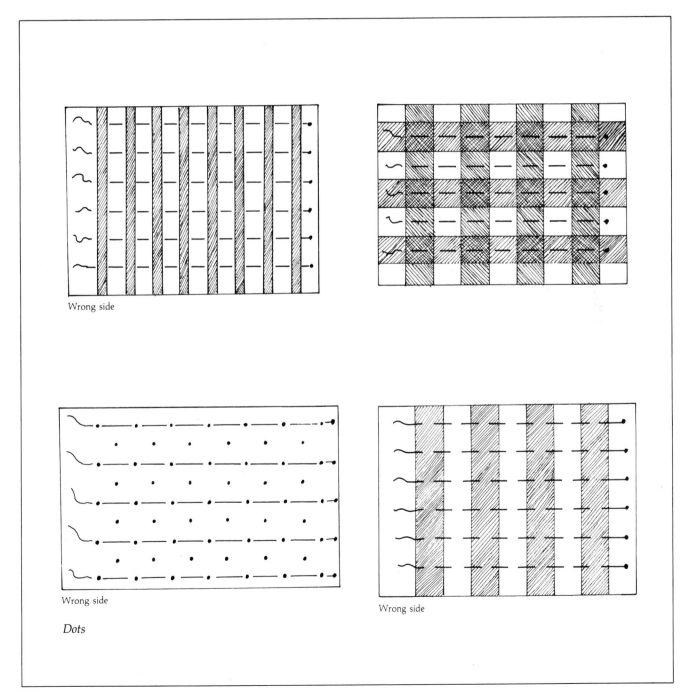

Wrong side

Wrong side

*Dots*

Wrong side

# Counterchange smocking

This is a simple form of smocking that can be worked on striped, dotted and checked fabrics without any preparation. It is sometimes called Mock Smocking, and is also known as Direct Smocking. It is basically Surface Honeycomb stitch or Vandyke stitch worked on the right side of the fabric.

Choose a fabric with a suitable size of stripe, dot or check, and one color of embroidery thread. The dramatic effect is caused by certain colors of the fabric being hidden in the smocking. This form of smocking is not as elastic as true smocking, so the exact width must be carefully calculated from a sampler.

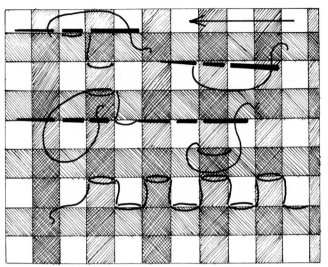

Right side

*Vandyke stitch worked on check fabric such as gingham. Striped fabrics can be worked the same way – rule faint lines as a guide to keep the stitching straight.*

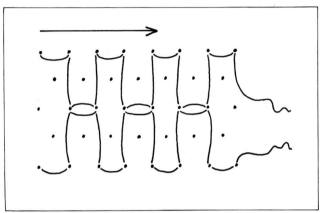

Right side

*Surface Honeycomb on dotted fabric*

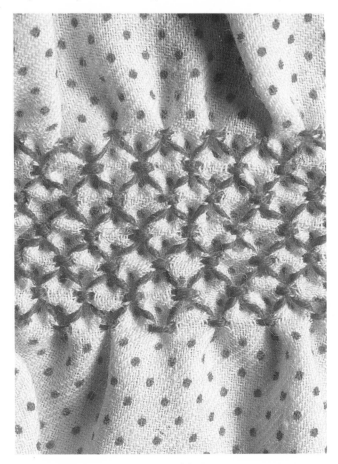

**Surface Honeycomb on dotted fabric.**
*By Gail Marsh.*

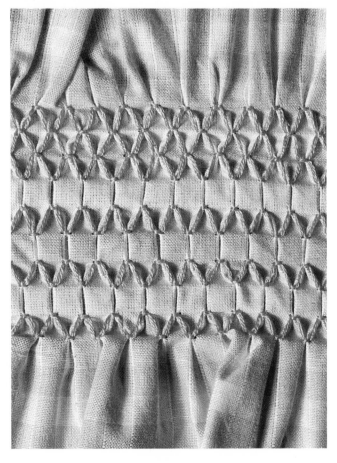

**Vandyke stitch on check fabric.** *By Gail Marsh.*

# Pleated fabrics

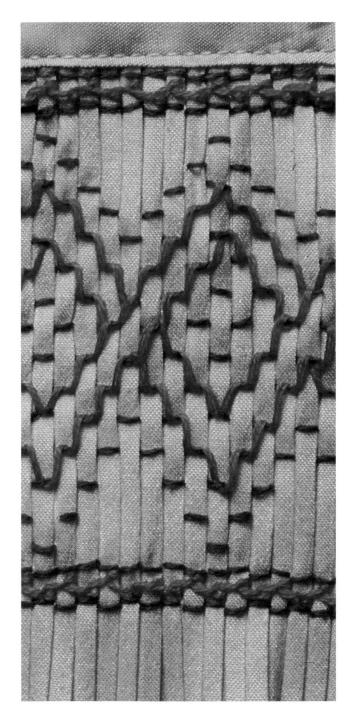

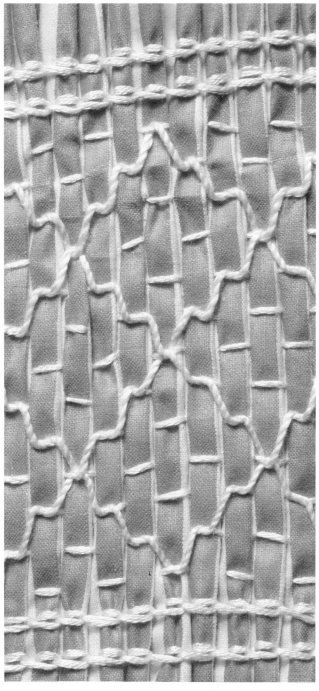

**Sample of permanently-pleated smocking.** *By Margaret Blow. A piece of permanently-pleated silk smocked in embroidery floss. The pleats are only ⅛in. (3mm) deep. The borders are rows of Double Running stitch – worked first one way and then back over the alternate pleats – enclosing a row of Feather stitching. The pleated area between is worked in spaced running stitches in a diamond pattern, accentuated by interlacing the stitches with a contrasting thread.*

**Sample of press-pleated smocking.** *By Margaret Blow. A cotton fabric with ⅕in. (5mm) wide stripes ironed into pleats showing only the darker color. It is smocked in cotton embroidery floss with two rows of Single Feather stitch at top and bottom. Alternative even rows of running stitch across the pleats are interlaced with diagonal rows of pearl cotton, to form a diamond pattern.*

# *To scale up a pattern graph*

One square represents 1sq.in. (2.5cm) on all the graphs in this book. Use ready squared pattern paper, which can be bought in either Imperial or Metric measures from art or stationery stores. Check whether seam allowance is included in the pattern.

**Transferring straight lines.** Start by marking out a straight edge of a pattern piece such as a center back fold line, counting the squares covered on the graph, and then marking along the same number on the squared pattern paper.

**Transferring curved lines.** Make a dot at the point in each square where the line crosses, noting whether it is a half or a quarter way along the line. Join up these points with a continuous curved line, adjusting it slightly if necessary to make an even curve.

**Check overall finished lengths and widths** with personal measurements, and draw in any necessary alterations.

**Put in balance marks** – center the front or back fold lines, grain lines, O's and any other information on graph.

**Check seam allowance** – as this may vary with different patterns. If it is not already included in the pattern, it can either be marked around the pattern piece before cutting out, or be allowed for when cutting out.

**Check required number of pieces to be cut** – such as four yokes, and mark this clearly on the pattern piece.

## Cutting out

Lay the pattern pieces out on the fabric as economically as possible, noting which pieces should be cut to a fold, or laid diagonally, and pin them in place.

Mark centers and balance marks, pleats etc., with tailor tacks. Cut the pieces out, and mark the boundaries of the smocked areas with a water-soluble pen or a line of basting.

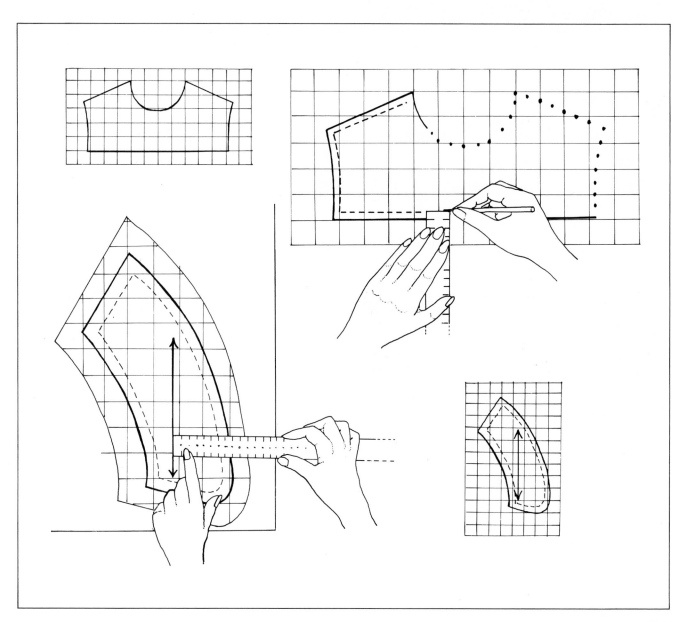

# Blue linen short smock

This is an adaptation of the traditional smock for casual wear – the fabric is linen and the smocking is worked in three shades of blue. Lines of stitching are worked around the collar and the shoulder-line to link up the areas of smocking, and three decorative buttons fasten the front opening.

**Size.** This pattern fits sizes 8 to 12. Seam allowances are ⅝in. (15mm), the hem allowance is 1½in. (4cm). The smock measures 30in. (76cm) from neck to hem.

**Fabric and materials.** 3yds (2.80m) of 36in. (90cm) medium-weight linen or linen-type. 2 balls each of light, medium- and dark-toned monochrome pearl cotton no. 5 for the smocking and embroidery. Sewing thread. Five self-cover button molds just over ½in. (15mm) diameter.

**Pattern.** The scale is one square to 1in. (2.5cm). Scale up the pattern as shown on page 30. Pin the pattern to the fabric, following the grain lines accurately and placing the collar, the center back yoke and the center back and center front lower smock pieces on the fold.

Cut out also, marking all the seam lines and the fold lines, the large O's, the balance marks, and the pleat and buttonhole positions. Use tailor-tacking or water soluble pen or chalk. Neaten the raw edges of the lower front and lower back pieces and the two sleeves with oversewing or machine Zigzag stitch – otherwise they may fray while being smocked. Stay-stitch around the front and back neck seamlines to prevent stretching.

**Smocking dots.** The dots and the rows should be ¼in. (6mm) apart. Use a smocking transfer and iron the dot pattern on to the back of the fabric.

**Smocked areas.** The areas to be gathered are only just over half the finished widths, and so the tubes have to be fairly close together. Pull up the gathering threads to approximately seven-eighths of the finished widths, which are as follows:
Back smock: 4¼in. (10.5cm);
Front smock: 11in. (28cm);
Top sleeve: 4in. (10cm);
Lower sleeve: 2¾in. (7cm).

**Smocking.** Start with the lightest shade of thread, and finishing with the darkest, work the smocking as follows, adapting to the different sizes and shapes of the smocked area:
1. Three rows of Outline stitch, two forming a Rope, and one in the same direction
2. Space
3. Ten rows of Cable stitch, forming a Basket pattern
4. Space
5. Two rows of Outline stitch in the same direction
6. Two rows of Wave/Trellis – forming a Chevron pattern
7. Three rows of Outline stitch, two in a rope and one in the same direction
8. Space
9. Four rows of Cable stitch, forming a Basket pattern
10. Four rows of Wave/Trellis, forming a Chevron pattern

## Embroidery

This can be done while assembling the smock (Method 1) or when the smock is finished (Method 2).

**Method 1.** *Yoke area:* after yoke has been sewn to lower smock and sleeves, and before the lining is hemmed down. *Collar:* before collar is attached to yoke. *Cuff:* after the top sides have been sewn to the sleeves and before the facing sides are hemmed down. *Pocket:* all lines, except the outer line, before making up. The outer line is sewn after the pockets are machined to the smock, hiding the machined lines.

**Method 2.** This is more tedious to work but enables the embroidered areas to be seen in relation to the whole. Work the stitches through the top layer of fabric only, sliding the needle between the layers. Work the yoke, collar and cuffs on the finished smock. Make up the pockets ready for attachment and then work the embroidered lines, except for the outer edge which is worked as Method 1.

Use the same threads as for smocking, and make bold lines of Twisted Chain, Twisted Chain with lacing, Whipped and Laced Holbein, Coral stitch, and Spanish Knotted Feather.

**Stitch.** Holbein is a double-running stitch. Lacing is the interlacing of a thread through the stitching from top to bottom then bottom to top; and whipping is the overcasting of the stitch with another thread.

### Pattern of embroidered lines

Twisted Chain stitch

Coral stitch

Spanish Knotted Feather stitch

## MAKING UP THE SMOCK

### Front opening band

1. With right sides together pin, baste and machine the long sides of the front bands to each side of the lower front smock front opening, matching O's and stopping at lower O. Trim the seams, snip towards the lower O, and fold the facing-side to the inside. Turn in the raw edges parallel to the foldline, pin, baste and hem to the previously machined lines. Again stop at the lower O.

Turn in the raw edges of the V-shaped lower tab on the outside of the smock. Trim the edges, clip into the corners, and press and baste into an evenly balanced V with very slightly rounded corners. Baste into position from O to O. Do the same with the tab shape on the inside of the smock. Sew the two facing-sides together so that the raw edges are not exposed. Baste the two tab shapes together through all thicknesses, from O around the V up to the second O; and across the band, back to the first O.

2. This can now be either machined or strongly stab-stitched, through all thicknesses. If the fabric is springy, as with linens

or synthetics, the remaining front band seams and folded edges can be top-stitched by machine or by hand for a firm, crisp edge.

## Yoke

Join the shoulder seams of the front and back yokes, and repeat on the lining pieces, matching the balance marks and easing the back on to the front. Press the seams open. Lay the composite yoke over the composite yoke lining, right sides together, and sew the front edges together from the center front balance marks, around the small section of neck seam, and down each front edges. Clip into the seams at the center front, and trim the edges of the stitched seam, clipping the corners off. Turn out these two front edges and press. Lay the whole yoke out flat and then baste the lining to the yoke around the neck seam, from center front to center front. Machine along this line.

## Collar

Fold the collar in half lengthwise (along the original fold line) with right sides together, and stitch down each end. Trim seams, clip corners and turn right side out. Press well.

## Collar and yoke

Matching center back, shoulder and center front balance marks, pin and baste the underside of the collar to the yoke through the neck seam. Machine along the neck seam. Trim the seams, clipping where necessary for a smooth line, and press the seams towards the collar. Turn under the raw edge of the upper collar neck seam, and hem it down along the previously machined line.

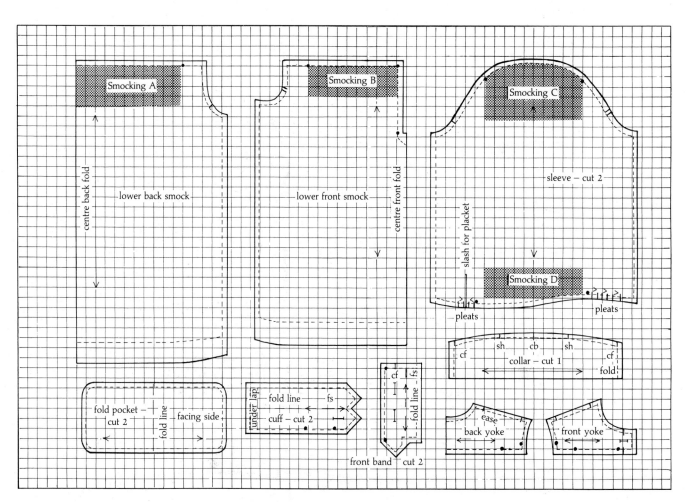

**Chart for classic short smock.** *By Bryony Nielsen.*

### Join yoke to lower smock

As machining will flatten the tubes, sew the seams as follows: turn under the lower raw edge of the outer back yoke, press and baste into position above the smocked edge of the lower back smock from O to O working on the right side. Using very small stitches, slip-stitch the edge of the yoke to the top of each tube. Now turn to the inside, undo the basting, and finish the seam by machining from O to armhole on each side, stitching along the pressed line on the outer back yoke. Sew each half of the front to the lower front smock, using the same method and matching O's and center fronts.

### Sleeve plackets

Cut two strips of fabric 1½in. × 6½in. (3.5cm × 16cm). Slash the marked placket lines on the sleeve, and spread the opening so that the slashed lines nearly form a straight line. Pin and baste the edge of one strip to this opening with right sides together and with the seam line running parallel to the raw edge of the strip, but tapering from less than ¼in. (4mm) to

**Classic short smock.** *By Bryony Nielsen. A useful garment with added lines of stitching which can be made in many fabrics. The detailed pattern opposite can be adapted for different fabrics and lengths.*

nearly nothing at the point on the sleeve. Machine along this line, being careful to avoid forming a small pleat at the apex of the opening. Press the seams onto the strip side, turn under the raw edges on the other side of the strip, and hem down to the back of the machined line. Repeat on the other sleeve.

**Join sleeves to smock**

Pin one sleeve to one armhole of the smock, matching O's and balance marks and easing the sleeves between these two marks on front and back. Baste and machine each side of the armhole seam from under-arm to smocking, and hand-sew to the tubes, as described above. Repeat this process on the other sleeve.

Lay the smock out flat, wrong side up. Turn under the raw edges of the yoke lining and pin them down to the previously sewn seams – along one half front, around one armhole, along the back, around the other armhole and along the second half front. All the raw edges are now encased between the yoke and the yoke lining. Hem the lining into position, being careful not to flatten the tubes.

Pin the side seams and under-arm seams together right sides facing and matching the under-arm seams. Baste and machine these seams in two continuous lines on each side of the smock. Press the seams open.

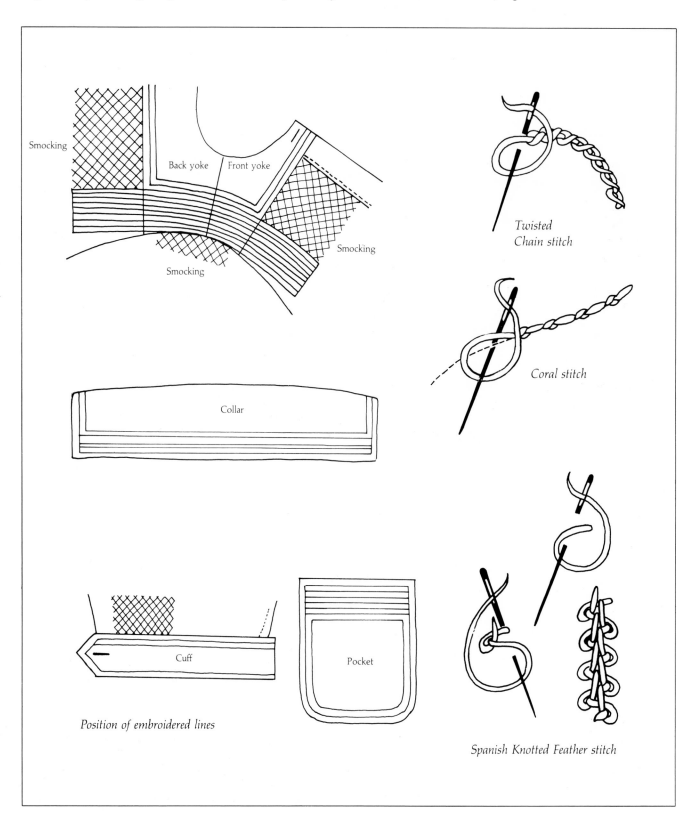

Smocking

Back yoke | Front yoke

Smocking

Smocking

*Twisted Chain stitch*

*Coral stitch*

Collar

Cuff

Pocket

*Position of embroidered lines*

*Spanish Knotted Feather stitch*

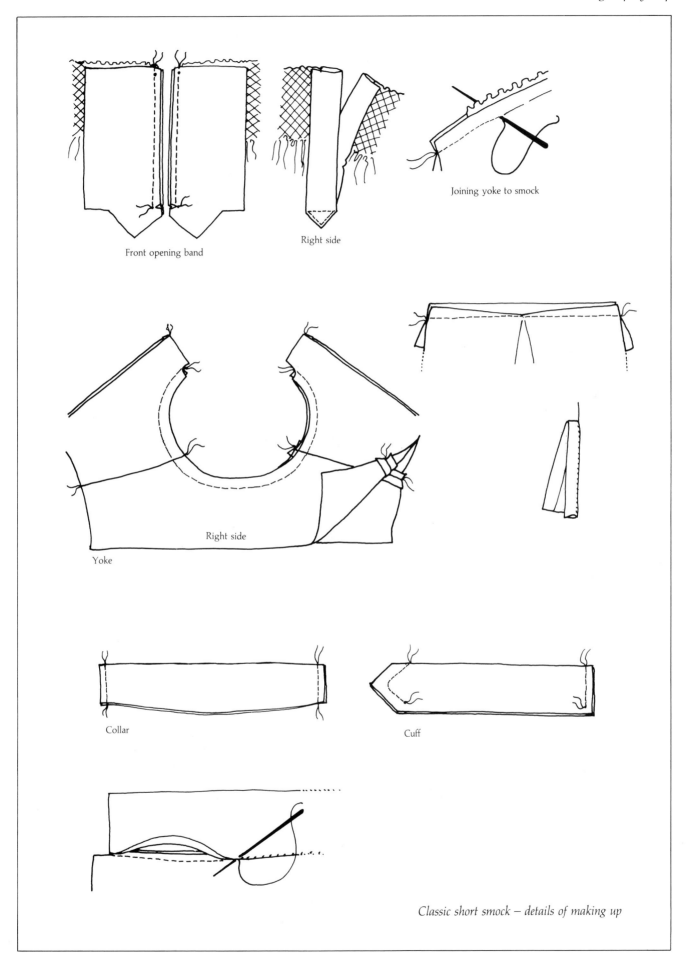

Front opening band

Right side

Joining yoke to smock

Yoke

Right side

Collar

Cuff

*Classic short smock – details of making up*

## Cuffs

Fold the cuff in half through the fold line, right sides together, stitch down the square end, and stitch around the pointed end (forming a very slightly rounded point), finishing off the machining firmly about ½in. (12mm) from the raw edge. Trim seams, clip corners, turn right side out and press well. Repeat this process on the other cuff.

Pin the remaining raw edge of the top side of the cuff to the lower edge of the sleeve, matching O's, and with the underlap extended ¾in. (18mm) beyond the placket opening. Using a combination of hand and machine sewing, join one cuff to one sleeve. Repeat for the other sleeve and cuff. Turn the sleeve inside out, turn under the raw edge of the facing side of the cuff, and hem it down to the back of the previously sewn seam. Slip-stitch the bottom of the underlap edges together. Repeat on the other cuff and sleeve.

## Buttons and buttonholes

Using the guide that comes with self-cover buttons, cut six circles of fabric. Cover a spare button with one of the circles and mark around the circumference where the base fits. Undo the button and mark all the circles with a similar circumference. From the edge of this circle to the center sew the ribs of a woven wheel. Center the wheel over the mold and fix in place. Complete the woven wheel. Work the buttonholes in matching thread.

## Pockets

Fold one pocket piece in half through the fold line with right sides together, and stitch all around, leaving a small opening for pulling through. Trim the seams, clip the corners, pull through, and press well. Repeat with the other pocket. Baste the pockets into position on the smock, and top-stitch the edges through all thicknesses with the machine.

## Hem

Turn up the hem and slip-stitch in place.

# CHAPTER 3

# *Traditional smocking on children's clothes*

# Smocking for children

Smocking on children's garments is both practical and decorative. The practical advantage is that the elasticity of the gathers gives room for movement and for growth, and the smocking can be as decorative as you like, both in the variety of stitches and the imaginative use of color.

Baby clothes with smocking have always been popular for both sexes, but today boys are unlikely to wear smocked suits beyond the age of four, although the styles change from gathered rompers to tailored-looking shorts with shirts.

Girls' dresses can be smocked in quite large sizes if the child still enjoys the appearance of such garments, and there is more scope for added decoration and trimmings than for the boys' outfits.

Fabrics should be of good quality and washable, as one of the requirements of a smocked garment is that it should 'grow with the child', and it may have to stand a good deal of wear.

Patterns are given for all the clothes shown in the photographs. These are in the form of charts on squared paper, and they should be scaled up to 1in. (2.5cm) squares unless otherwise noted. *All seams have been allowed, so the outline is the actual cutting line.* All yokes are double, with the gathers of the smocked panels completely hidden between the two layers. This adds both neatness and strength. A basic knowledge of simple dress-making is assumed, but details of attaching collars, making plackets and working with double yokes can be found at the back of this book.

The gauge for smocking the baby dresses and the romper suits illustrated is approximately 22 tubes to every 6in. (15cm) of fabric. On a shirt front it is 66 tubes on each half of a shirt

**Doll with a matching outfit.** *By May Williams. This doll has a complete outfit of dress, coat, hat, mittens and handbag, and zippered boots. Underneath her smocked dress she wears hand-embroidered lingerie.*

front, and the design must be calculated so that the pattern is identical either side of the band of fastening. Gathers must be accurately counted if you are going to work any embroidered motifs as well as the smocking.

Attention to detail is particularly important on small garments. Collars and cuffs can have embroidered edging in colors to match the smocking. Tiny four-hole pearl buttons look attractive if sewn on with the brightest shade used in the embroidery, and buttonholes look best if they are carefully done by hand. Small necks need accurately placed collars meeting in the exact center of the garments.

Suggestions for trimming the edge of collars and cuffs:
1. Herringbone stitch just in from the edge.
2. Blanket stitch in groups of three, a short stitch on either side of a long one.
3. Oversewing in one direction with one color, then the reverse way in a contrasting color (see gingham romper on page 54).
4. An evenly spaced row of French knots.

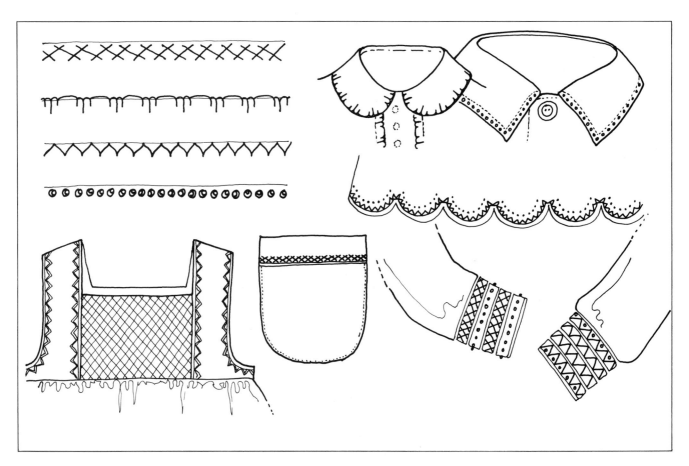

# Embroidered motifs on children's clothes

Motifs look very charming when spaced across smocking, and give much pleasure to the child who is wearing the garment. They can be designed to reflect hobbies or interests, or consist of such easily recognised shapes as boats, rabbits, trains, soldiers, cherries or flowers. The following instructions are for three simple shapes, and, once having mastered the technique, enthusiastic smockers will be able to use their creative skills to design their own motifs.

The motifs described below are worked mainly in cable stitch with the rows close together. Stitches must not be too

**Child's Round smock.** *By Sheila Sturrock. This smock is a half-size of a traditional Round smock, cut to the same pattern. It is made in poly-cotton and embroidered with coton à broder.*

tight or the smocking will lose its elasticity. Use a length of embroidery floss long enough to complete each color. Alternate rows are worked by turning the design upside down, so that you are always stitching from left to right.

## Rabbit

1.  Start with the bottom row using eight tubes.
2.  2nd row, add one stitch at each end (ten tubes).
3.  3rd row, increase again at each end.
4.  Continue for four more rows on these twelve stitches.
5.  Decrease at each end of consecutive rows until you are working on six tubes only.
6.  Four more rows will then form the head.
7.  Ears: continue for four more rows, taking the floss on to the wrong side between the third and fourth stitch of each row to separate them. Finish ears with a single stitch.
8.  Tail: embroider in satin stitch and add some stem stitches in green to represent the surrounding grass.

## Train

1.  Starting with the main color, work right along the length of the train.
2.  Work on ten tubes for the first truck, taking the cotton onto the wrong side at the tenth stitch and bringing it up into the eleventh tube. Carry on for the next truck in the same manner.
3.  The engine is worked on twelve tubes.
4.  After three rows of cable stitch have been completed along the length of the train, add two extra rows to the height of the engine, plus a funnel as in the diagram.
5.  Work a trail of smoke in stem stitch.
6.  The base of the train is one continuous row of cable stitch in a dark shade, with extra stitches to represent wheels and front of boiler.

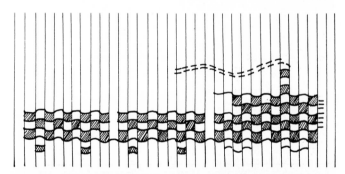

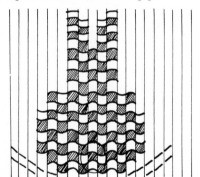

*Stitch diagrams for embroidered motifs.*

**Sample of a rabbit motif.** *By Mary Cornall.*

**Sample of a train motif.** *By Mary Cornall.*

# Silk christening gown

The deep band of smocking at the front of this christening gown has embroidered panels at each side, based on traditional feather stitch patterns. They could be designed to include family names or monograms, or traditional symbols such as hearts and flowers.

There is a deeply tucked hem, and a lining which helps the fabric to fall in rich folds. As it will only be worn at long intervals, the gown is stored on a hanger in a linen pillowcase, the front of which is embroidered with the names of the babies who have worn the gown.

**Size.** The gown measures 30in. (75cm) from neck to hem, and 12in. (30cm) across the embroidered and smocked panels on the front.

**Pattern.** This should be scaled up as described on page 30. However, the scale for this pattern is 1in. (2.5cm) to the square. The skirt consists of two pieces 36in. × 36in. (90cm × 90cm) in silk, and two pieces 26in. × 33in. (66cm × 84cm) in the lining fabric with the armholes cut out as shown. The seam allowance is ½in. (12mm) on side skirts and sleeve seams, and ¼in. (6mm) on all other pieces.

**Fabric.** 2½yds (2.30m) of 36in. (90cm) wide hand-washable spun silk, and 1¾yds (1.50m) of cotton lawn for the lining.

**Other materials.** 8 skeins of white embroidery floss (use three strands in the needle). 6 pearl buttons. 1 hook (work thread eye).

**Smocking dots.** Dots and rows ¼in. (6mm) apart. You could use a smocking dot transfer but if the dots show through to the right side of the fabric use the tissue basting method described on page 15.

## SMOCKED AREAS

**Front.** Place 16 rows of dots in the center, leaving 4in. (10cm) from the side seam each side for the embroidered area. Starting ¼in. (6mm) from the top, mark out the area for the embroidery in between the arm-hole and the dots.

**Back.** Mark the center, and leave a 2in. (5cm) space. Place six rows of dots each side, 1in. (2.5cm) from the arm-hole and a ¼in. (6mm) from the top edge.

**Sleeves.** Neaten the side edges. Turn under a ¾in. (18mm) hem at the cuffs, and sew. Place 6 rows of dots right across from seam to seam above the hem. Place 2 rows of dots across the top of the sleeve ½in. (12mm) from the top edge.

Stitch the gathers for the smocked areas and pull them up.

*Silk christening gown with embroidered panels.* By Pat Steward. *The smocking on the front is placed between two embroidered panels, the neck and cuffs are frilled and the skirt is lined to fall in heavy folds.*

## SMOCKING

**Front:** there are sixteen rows of gathers. Leave the top line and start on the second.

ROW 1. *Outline stitch*

ROW 2. *Double Cable stitch*

ROW 3. *Outline stitch*

ROW 4. *Diamond stitch*

ROW 5. *Crossed Diamond*

ROW 6. *Diamond stitch*

ROW 7. *Outline stitch*

ROW 8. *Feathered Diamond stitch* – to fill the space between the rows of Outline

ROW 9. *Outline stitch*

ROWS 10 to 12. *Crossed Diamond stitch (as rows 4–6)*

ROW 13. *Outline stitch*

ROW 14. *Vandyke stitch* – up to row 13

ROW 16. *Double Vandyke stitch* – from row 14 down

**Back:** there are six rows of gathers. Leave the top line and start on the second

ROW 1. *Outline stitch*

ROW 2. *Double Cable stitch*

ROW 3. *Outline stitch*

ROW 4. *Vandyke stitch* – up to row 3

ROW 5. *Double Vandyke stitch* – down from row 4

**Cuff:** there are six rows of gathers. Start on the first line

ROW 1. *Diamond stitch*

ROWS 2 to 4. *Crossed Diamond stitch*

ROW 5. *Diamond stitch*

**Sleeve top.** Work one row of Crossed Diamond stitch between the two rows of gathers.

When all the pieces are smocked, remove all gathering threads except the first two in the skirt section, and set the smocking as described on page 16.

## EMBROIDERY

The half-pattern shown is actual size. Trace it off and mark in the other half. Transfer the design to the fabric by one of the methods on pages 14–15. Using three strands in the needle, start with the central French knots, and then work the heart-shaped petals in Single Feather stitch. The scrolls are worked twice, in Single Feather stitch worked back to back. The tendrils are in Stem, and the border in Herringbone stitch.

**Chart for christening gown.** *By Pat Steward. The scale for this pattern is 1 in. (2.5cm) to the square.*

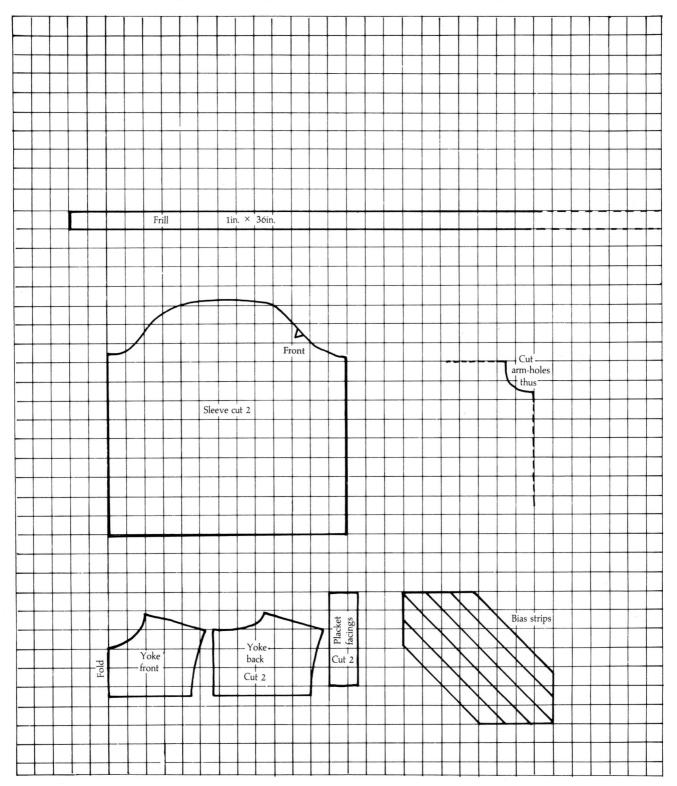

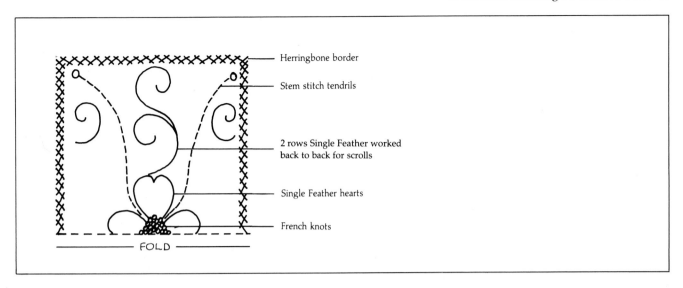

— Herringbone border

— Stem stitch tendrils

— 2 rows Single Feather worked back to back for scrolls

— Single Feather hearts

— French knots

FOLD

*Half-pattern for embroidered box*

## TO MAKE UP

Stitch the front yoke to the front skirt, right sides together and raw edges even.

**Placket:** cut 5in. (12.5cm) down the center of the back skirt. With the right sides together, place placket facings each side and sew close to the edge. Turn in on stitching, and hand-stitch in place on inside. Lap the right side over the left, forming a pleat below the placket, and stitch across.

Sew back silk yokes to cotton yokes along back edges. With right side facing and raw edges even, sew silk yokes to silk skirts.

Join silk yokes at shoulders. Join cotton yokes at shoulders. Join seams of each skirt and press open.

Cut back of cotton skirt down the center for 5½in. (14cm) and make a narrow hem. Gather the tops of lining to fit (leaving back placket of dress out). Sew cotton skirts to dress above the seam line; turn yoke facings in and stitch over the seams. Baste neck and arm-hole edges together.

**Frill.** Fold in half lengthways, and stitch along the short ends. Turn right side out and gather long edge through double thickness. Draw up to fit neck. Baste frill on outside, raw edges even. Place a bias strip over and sew together. Turn bias to inside and slip-stitch in place. Embroider a line of Double Feather stitch around the neck.

**Sleeves.** Sew sleeve seam and press open. Gather the top of the sleeve and adjust it to fit, with the most fullness at the top, and sew in place. The seam can be bound with bias strips to neaten it.

Finish the back opening with buttons and buttonholes, and one hook and eye at the neck.

**Hem.** Mark for tucks 6¼in. (16cm) from bottom edge, and make three more lines 1½in. (4.5cm) apart. Crease on the marks, and machine-stitch ½in. (12mm) in from the creases. Press down. Turn under ¼in. (6mm) on bottom edge, turn up to bottom pleat, and press. Embroider a line of Double Feather stitch just above the crease before stitching up the hem. Embroider a line of Double Feather stitch just on or below the machine line on the top tuck, and embroider the others in the same way with Stem stitch.

Turn up the hem on the petticoat and embroider all around with a line of Double Feather stitch.

# Christening gown

This gown is made in a soft washable spun silk, trimmed with frills, lace and ribbon. The smocking is gathered into a round yoke, and the sleeves are smocked around the cuffs.

**Size.** Ages 3–6 months. As the neck and yoke are the only fitted sections this gown could be worn by a child up to about one year. The length from neck to hem at the center back is 32in. (81cm).

**Pattern.** As graph. Scale up as shown on page 30.

**Fabric.** 3¼yd (3m) of pure spun silk 36in. (90cm) wide. Eyelet lace and ⅛in. (3mm) ribbon.

**Smocking dots.** A ¼in. (6mm) scale was used. If the fabric is washable, iron the dots on to the wrong side of the fabric in the usual way, sew the rows of gathers, and then wash the fabric to remove the dots before pulling up the threads. If the fabric is not washable, use the tissue transfer method (page 15).

**Smocked area.** The smocking is gathered into a fitted round yoke and finishes in points at the lower edge. Three straight rows of smocking on each sleeve are gathered to form a stretchy cuff at the wrist with a lace-edge frill.

**Silk christening gown with round yoke and chart.**
*By Ann Tranquillini. The full style will fit any baby and it can be trimmed with frills, lace and ribbons.*

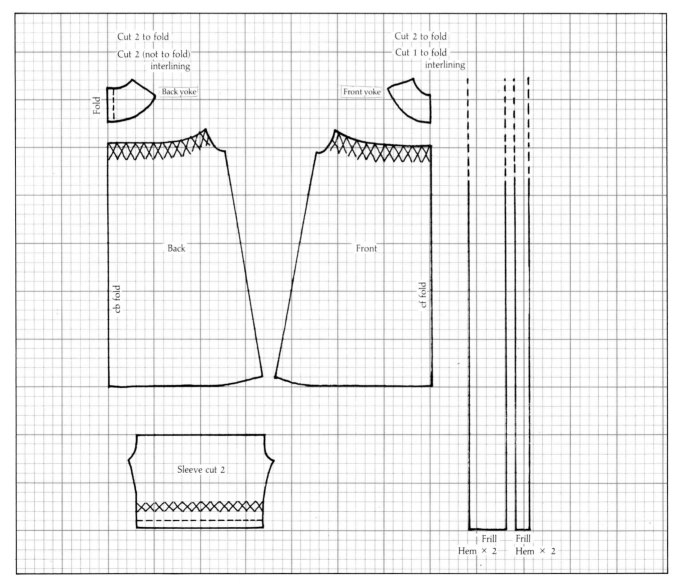

## ORDER OF WORK

1. Lay the pattern on the fabric. Cut out the pieces with ⅝in. (15mm) seam allowances.

2. The yoke needs three layers, an outer one, a lining or facing and an interlining, because seams will show through this fabric. All three can be cut from the same silk. The center back opening of the yoke is cut to a fold line (outer layer and lining being one). The interlining is basted inside to this fold line.

3. Slash and shape dot transfer or tissue to fit the circular yoke. Cut out section for cuffs. Transfer dots to fabric (see page 16 for joining dots at seams).

4. Join sleeve seams to front and back.

5. Pull up and secure the gathers round the yoke line.

6. Mark a small gap at the center back for an opening.

7. Work three complete rows of Honeycomb stitch around the yoke in silk thread or embroidery floss, using two strands in the needle. Start to the left of the marked gap and finish at the right. Work the pointed edge as follows: start at center front and work the stitch on the three central groups; turn the work the other way up and stitch two groups in the opposite direction; turn the work again and stitch the last group, forming a point. Thread the needle back through the folds to work the next point, continuing to the center back.

8. Start again at the center front and work in the opposite direction to complete the other half of the yoke. Try to even up the points so that they match at the center back opening, if necessary making an extra fold in the opening.

9. Join side seams of dress, and sleeve under-arms.

10. Stitch lace to fold line of cuff frill, turn up the frill on this line and hem to a line between the first and second rows of gathers. Pull up the gathers and smock around sleeve without leaving a gap, working three rows of Honeycomb stitch. Remove all gathers.

11. Remove all gathers on yoke except for the top row. Pull out the smocking, and shape it to fit the yoke. Steam on the wrong side to set the size (page 16).

12. Make a continuous strip opening at center back in gap left in smocking.

13. Prepare the layers of the yoke by laying the outer yoke over the interlining of the front yoke and basting them together. Then treat as one. The back yoke is cut to a fold at the opening edge, one part being the outer layer and the other part being the lining or facing. The interlining is cut only to this fold line and is invisibly stitched there. Stitch the shoulder seams through the double layers. Stitch the shoulder seams of the lining or facing sections.

14. Strengthen the button and buttonhole areas with a strip of ironed-on interfacing.

15. Set yoke onto smocking, hem the lining or facing yoke over the gathers to neaten the inside.

16. Baste lace frill along the neck seam line. Bind the neck edge over all layers of yoke and frill of lace with a bias strip of silk.

17. Work buttonholes and sew on buttons.

18. Make up the rest of the dress with frills and lace as desired. An eyelet lace is very pretty with a ribbon threaded through and a few tiny bows.

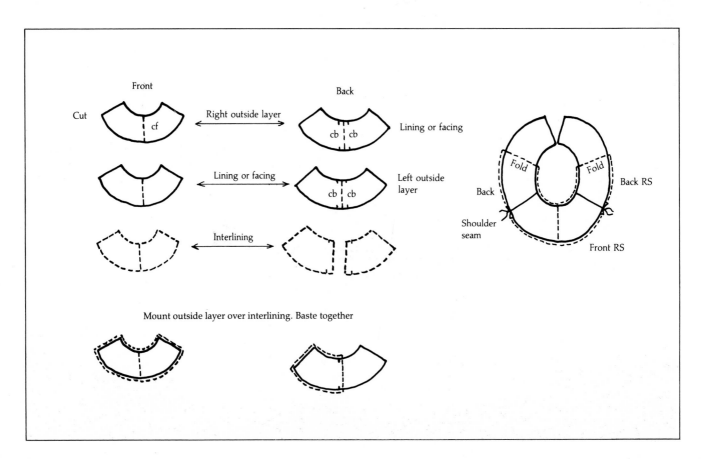

**Dress and bonnet.** *By Olive Camplin. A simple outfit, finely worked on pink checked cotton with matching smocking.*

**Dress with collar.** *By Olive Camplin. A practical party dress in blue and white striped nylon with shaded smocking.*
**Dress with sleeves.** *By Olive Camplin. Another party dress in white nylon with a neat insert of blue smocking, with matching smocking on the sleeves and a line of blue stitchery around the neck.*
**Smocked drawstring bag.** *By Rachel Newall. Striped cotton smocked in red and blue, finished with a tassel.*

**Round-yoke baby dress.** *By Mary Cornall. This summer dress is delicately smocked in a light and airy fabric. For this type of yoke only use very fine fabrics, as the smocking stitches have to be much tighter on the neck edge than on the outer rows of the pattern to give an adequate curve.*

# Baby dress

This exquisite little dress is made of fine white cotton voile, and would be ideal for a new baby.

**Size.** 14in. (36cm) from neck to hem.

**Pattern.** As chart – each square represents 1sq.in. (2.5 sq.cm). Scale up as shown on page 30.

**Fabric.** 1¼ yds (1.10m) of fine cotton or silk. Lace edging if desired.

**Threads.** Two shades of yellow embroidery floss, with four strands in the needle for the smocking.

**Smocking dots.** 7 rows of dots ⅜in. (9mm) apart. Marked by dot transfer on the back or gathered by smocking machine.

**Baby dress and chart.** *By Mary Cornall. A delicate dress in pale colors for a tiny girl.*

**Smocked area.** The dress is smocked to a depth of 2in. (5cm) front and back, with a 4in. (10cm) placket at the back for the button.

**Smocking.** Choosing a small design, working at least two rows between each row of gathers. Large diamonds or widely spaced rows are not suitable for such a delicate little dress.

## ORDER OF WORK

This is the same as for the dress on page 62, except that the neck and the sleeves are finished with a narrow binding, and lace can be added if required.

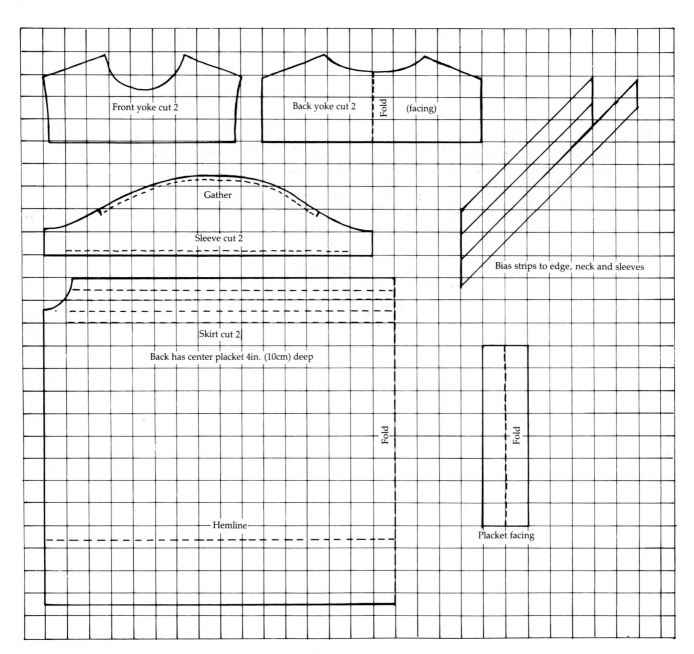

**Blue sundress.** *By May Williams. Made in a Laura Ashley cotton print, the dress is made of 2 × 36in. (91cm) widths of fabric. The yoke is a straight double strip back and front, enclosing the smocking. Straps are inserted when the yoke is made up. A curved shape is cut to accommodate the arm-hole shaping, which should be faced with a strip of fabric.*

*The smocking is worked in the same stitches as the pink dress in crochet cotton to blend with the print, and needle lace is worked round the whole of the top.*

**Pink check dress.** *By May Williams. Made of checked gingham, embroidered in two tones of pink coton à broder. 1 × 36in. (91cm) width is used for the back and one for the front, which is smocked right across to a depth of 5in. (13cm). A double yoke is used, and the sashes are enclosed in the under-arm seams. The smocking stitches include Stem, Chevron and Diamond stitch, and the stitching picks up only the pink squares on the tubing.*

*Needle lace is worked directly round the neck and arm-holes, and the back fastens with hand-made Dorset buttons.*

# All-in-one romper

This gingham romper has a half belt at the back and plenty of fullness, making it a comfortable outfit for an active baby.

**Size.** Suitable for ages 6 months to 1 year.

**Pattern.** As chart. Each square represents 1sq.in. (2.5cm). Draw the pattern to scale as described on page 30.

**Fabric.** 1¼yd (1.10m) of blue checked gingham.

**Threads.** Embroidery floss in deep blue and white, and a contrast color for the motif. Use four strands in the needle for the smocking.

**Smocked area.** Front only, 1in. (2.5cm) at yoke and waistline (position marked on chart).

**Smocking dots.** Gingham can be gathered accurately by using the squares as a guideline. There should be 11 tubes to every 3in. (7.5cm).

**Smocking.** Work a close design, otherwise the waistline band will stretch in wear. The romper is shown with boat motifs (instructions at end of chapter on page 64).

*All-in-one romper and chart.* By Mary Cornall. *Two bands of smocking hold in the fullness of this little romper, with embroidered boats to add interest.*

## ORDER OF WORK

Attach placket facing in the center back, then gather each side to fit the back yokes. Insert each belt piece level with the waistline smocking as the side seams are joined, and attach a button for fastening. Proceed with yokes, collars and cuffs as for the dress on page 62, but on this garment there are three buttons on the back yoke and none on the placket.

Join the crotch facings to the garment before stitching the leg hems. Insert 11in. (28cm) of elastic to these hems, making sure that the ends are secure. Work three buttonholes on the front, and sew the buttons onto the double material of the back facing (shown in more detail on the Buster Romper chart on page 56). Or, attach three heavy-duty snaps in place of buttons and buttonholes.

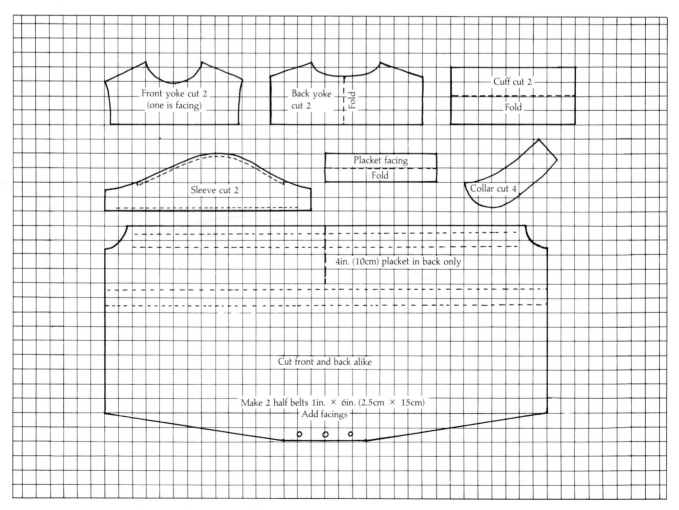

Front yoke cut 2 (one is facing)

Back yoke cut 2 — Fold

Cuff cut 2 — Fold

Sleeve cut 2

Placket facing Fold

Collar cut 4

4in. (10cm) placket in back only

Cut front and back alike

Make 2 half belts 1in. × 6in. (2.5cm × 15cm)
Add facings

# Buster romper

This is a very practical suit for a baby boy as it will fit until he is out of diapers. The large tuck in the shirt allowance means that the buttons can be lowered as the child grows. Easy changing is facilitated by the between-leg fastening. Many fabrics would be suitable – this romper is in Viyella.

**Size.** 16in.–18in. (41cm–46cm), adjustable.

**Pattern.** The chart for the trouser pattern is shown here. The seam allowance of ⅜in. (9mm) is included. The shirt pattern is the same as that for the 'Bocker' suit on page 60. Each square represents 1sq.in. (2.5sq.cm). Scale up (page 30).

**Fabric.** ¾yd (0.70m) of white and ⅔yd (0.60m) of blue, both in either cotton or fine wool.

**Threads.** Embroidery floss in a shade to match the blue fabric, with four strands in the needle for the smocking.

**Smocked areas.** 7 rows of dots ⅜in. (9mm) apart. Mark with dot transfer or gather with a smocking machine.

**Smocking.** Work rows 1 and 7 in a Double Cable stitch to make a neat border. Work a diamond design for the center. Make sure that the design is identical on each side of the center panel.

*Buster romper and chart. By Mary Cornall. A warm and practical suit which can be lengthened by moving the buttons.*

## ORDER OF WORK

### Shirt

Join each front smocked panel to a single yoke. Join shoulder seam of yoke onto the back of the shirt. Use yoke facings to neaten both these seams on the inside of the shirt. Stitch on the front buttonhole panels. Join side seams and oversew. Stitch the sleeve seams and make a 2in. (5cm) hem which turns back into a cuff. Make the collar, with a ¼in. (6mm) seam allowance, and edge with colored stitchery (see page 38). Stitch the cuffs to match. Attach the collar to the neck edge with a narrow bias strip. Stitch the sleeves into arm-holes and oversew seams to neaten. Turn up a small hem on the lower edge of the shirt.

Work five buttonholes on the front panel approximately 2in. (5cm) apart – the first one being close to the neck edge and central to the collar. Sew on buttons.

### Trousers

Stitch side seams to within 2½in. (6cm) of the waist. Gather the waist to fit the band, and attach each band, hemming on the inside to neaten. Work four buttonholes on each band (positions marked on chart). The buttonholes at each end of the front band overlap the ends of the back band and button onto the side seam of the shirt. Finish the legs as for the gingham romper on page 54.

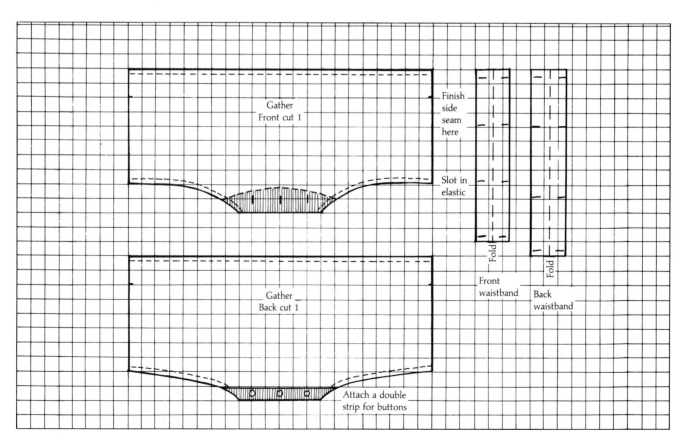

Gather
Front cut 1

Finish side seam here

Slot in elastic

Fold

Fold

Front waistband

Back waistband

Gather
Back cut 1

Attach a double strip for buttons

# Buster suit

An outfit for a party or a very special occasion, this suit has a cream silk smocked shirt and red velvet trousers.

**Size.** 18in.–20in. (46cm–51cm) length, for ages 2–3 years.

**Pattern.** As chart. Each square represents 1sq.in. (2.5sq.cm). Draw the pattern to scale as described on page 30.

**Fabric.** ⅞yd (0.80m) of silk (or fine cotton) for the shirt. ½yd (0.40m) of velvet for the shorts. ⅓yd (0.30m) cotton for shorts lining.

**Smocked area.** The front of the shirt is smocked on each side of the front panel to a depth of 2½in. (6cm).

**Smocking dots.** 8 rows of dots ⅜in. (9mm) apart. Mark by dot transfer on the back, or gather by machine.

**Smocking.** A bold design of scallops and diamonds.

**Row 1.** Work scallops between rows 1 and 2 with 12 stitches forming each loop. Row 2 is straight cable stitch. Diamonds are worked with row 3 in the center, 6 stitches forming each one, so that two diamonds fit below each scallop. Reverse

these rows between 6, 7 and 8. The center diamonds between 4 and 5 can be larger or double.

**Buster suit and chart.** *By Mary Cornall. A smart silk shirt with deep bands of smocking, matching the velvet trousers.*

## ORDER OF WORK

Make up the shirt in the same way as the shirt of the buster romper.

### Shorts

Stitch darts, tucks and all seams on the velvet. Stitch the lining seams. Place lining inside shorts with the seams facing. Baste the edge of the leg lining to the edge of the velvet in the finished position. The shorts can then be turned through and stitched by machine, for strength. As the lining is shorter than the velvet the leg does not need hemming; the turning stays back in position. Turn the velvet over 1½in. (4cm) at the waistline. Work the buttonholes through the double fabric. Hand-sew the lining to the remaining edges of waist and placket. Make the belt.

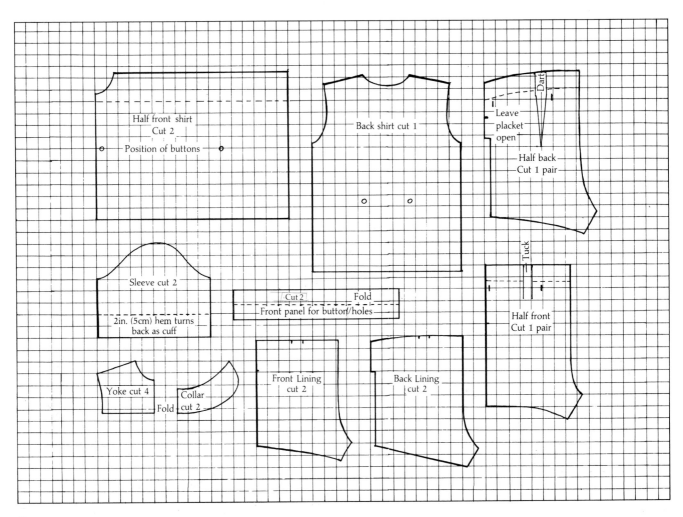

# 'Bocker' suit with car motif

A bocker suit is designed for the in-between stage when a child is walking but still wearing diapers. The shorts have a neat front, but there is elastic at the back of the leg to disguise the diaper.

The fabric is Swiss cotton, white for the shirt and royal blue for the shorts. The color of the smocking matches the shorts, and a motif of a boat, car or train would delight any small boy.

**Size.** 16in.–18in. (41cm–46cm), adjustable by moving shirt buttons. Age 1–2 years.

**Pattern.** As chart. Each square represents 1sq.in. (2.5sq.cm). Draw the pattern to scale as shown on page 30.

**Fabric.** ¾yd (0.70m) white cotton for shirt. ½yd (0.40m) of royal blue cotton for shorts, and ⅓yd (0.30m) of fine lawn lining.

**Threads.** Embroidery floss in royal blue and red – four strands in the needle for the smocking.

**Smocked areas.** The shirt is smocked each side of the front panel to a depth of 2in. (5cm).

**Bocker suit and chart.** *By Mary Cornall. This crisp looking cotton suit has embroidered motifs as well as smocking, both matching the color of the trousers.*

**Smocking dots.** 7 rows of dots ⅜in. (9mm) apart. Mark by dot transfer or gather by machine.

**Smocking.** The first two rows are royal blue Cable stitch, with Surface Honeycomb between them in red. A similar border is worked between rows 6 and 7. Calculate the center to work a motif in red (motifs on pages 40–1). Fill in either side of the motif with Honeycomb stitch in blue, or small diamonds.

## ORDER OF WORK

Make the shirt exactly the same as for the buster romper shirt on page 56. The shorts are made as for the buster suit on page 58, with the following exception: when the leg edge lining has been joined to the main fabric, make a row of running stitches parallel to the join from the side seam across to the inside leg seam, and slot in a 5½in. (14cm) length of elastic.

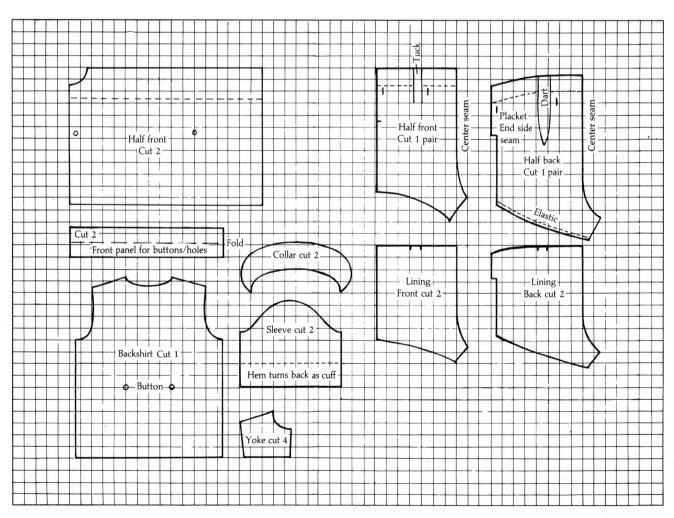

# White dress embroidered with cherries

This fresh and pretty dress is made in fine white Swiss cotton, and pairs of embroidered cherries decorate the bodice in between the rows of smocking. The collar and cuffs are edged with cherry red.

**Size.** 20in. (51cm) from neck to hem.

**Pattern.** As chart, each square represents 1sq.in. (2.5sq.cm). Draw the pattern to scale as described on page 30. The skirt is two complete widths of 36in. (90cm) fabric, each cut 21in. (53cm) long, allowing 3½in. (9cm) hem. There is a 4/10in. (10mm) seam allowance on yokes, shoulders and arm-holes, and ¼in. (6mm) on collars, plackets and facings.

**Fabric.** 1¾yd (1.50m) of good quality pure cotton.

**Threads.** Red embroidery floss. Use 4 strands in the needle for the smocking, and 3 for the embroidery.

**Smocking dots.** 16 rows of dots ⅜in. (9mm) apart. These can be marked on the back with a dot transfer, or gathered by smocking machine.

**Smocked area.** The dress is smocked both front and back with a central button panel at the back. Work the back smocking in two equal halves, leaving 1¾in. (4.5cm) gap in the center for the opening. The smocking is 5½in. (14cm) deep and shaped at the arm-holes.

**Smocking.** Work the smocking on the front first, and then continue on the back starting from the side seams and working towards the center, so as to calculate the placket area.

**Front.** Start work 2in. (5cm) from the edge so as to shape the arm-hole, increasing one stitch each end of the next five rows.

**ROW 1.** The scallop design is worked between the first and second row. Count the gathers in order to find the center – each 'loop' takes ten stitches.

*Dress with cherries. By Mary Cornall. An enchantingly pretty cotton dress decorated with pairs of cherries across the bodice in between the smocking.*

**ROW 2.** Straight row of Cable stitch. This design is repeated between rows 4 and 5, the scallops being in exact reverse. The cherries are worked in small groups of Cable stitch on row 3, linked by stalks in green Straight stitch.

**ROWS 6–11.** The central block of smocking is in Surface Honeycomb, and the border of cherries is repeated between rows 12 and 16.

## ORDER OF WORK

### Make the back placket

Make a cut 7in. (18cm) deep and ¼in. (6mm) away from the left side of the work, and attach a placket facing the entire length of the opening. Work the buttonholes through the facing.

### Double yokes

Join the four shoulder seams and press them flat, so that the turnings are facing each other. Join the front yoke to the front smocking, being careful to center it. Hem the facing on to the gathers to neaten the inside. Attach the back yokes in the same way.

### Collars and cuffs

Make collars with ¼in. (6mm) seams, and embroider the edge before attaching it to the neck. Neaten the neck with a narrow bias strip. Stitch the seam of the cuffs and fold them in half, work embroidery to match the collar along the fold. The cuff turns back again after it is attached to the gathered sleeve.

Gather the top of the sleeves and fit them into the arm-holes. Fasten the back of the neck with two small hooks and bars. Turn up the skirt and hem.

*Each back yoke is folded in half on the dotted line, and when the garment is finished one side overlaps the other, so it needs to be larger.*

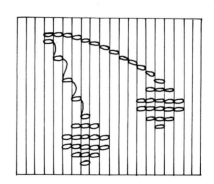

*Stitch diagram for cherry motif*

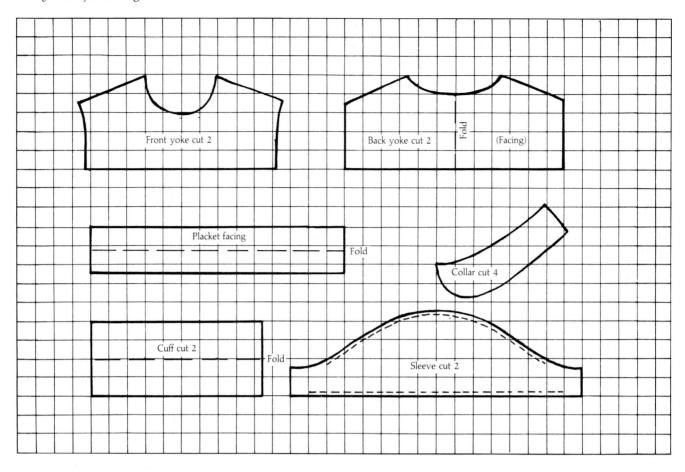

**Chart for dress with cherries.** *By Mary Cornall.*

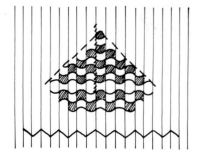

**Boat**

1. Start with the bottom row using eight tubes.
2. 2nd row is worked on ten tubes (1 extra each end).
3. 3rd row is worked on twelve tubes (1 extra each end).
4. Change color for the sails.
5. 1st row is twelve tubes for hull.
6. At each end of consecutive rows, reduce by one stitch and a triangular shape will form.
7. Edge the triangle with stem stitch to give a well-defined outline.
8. Embroider a mast in a contrasting color.
9. A 'wavy' line of smocking looks most appropriate below the boat.

# CHAPTER 4

# *Fashion smocking*

# Smocking in Fashion

Famous couturiers often use embroidery techniques to give their clothes the detail and interesting texture that makes their designs individual and of high quality.

The use of smocking in fashion design is not at all complicated; as you can see from the charming, comfortable and easily assembled clothes in the following pages, smocking can be used on highly fashionable clothes as well as the more classic and timeless designs.

It is one of the easiest hand-embroidery techniques to adapt to dress, as it is concerned with the manipulation of fabric. The shape and placing of smocked areas can be used to give shadows or highlights as well as color and pattern, and the released fullness will enhance the style line.

## DESIGN

Traditionally smocks were based on the mathematical division of hand-woven cloth into rectangles of various sizes (as explained on page 10) where no scrap of fabric was wasted. Today the wealth of fashion fabrics available is an inspiration in itself, and many a good design idea has sprung from a fascination with a beautiful textile.

Smocking can add a texture to a surface: it can change the color; impose a new pattern; alter the weight; catch the light; or form deep honeycombs of shadow. Released fullness can spring into sculptured outline or flow closely over the figure. Any or all of these aspects of smocking may be used in a fashion design, and many of them depend entirely on the type of fabric chosen.

What sparks off a design? A fashion drawing perhaps, a fabric, a color, a pattern, a technique, or the need to make something for a special occasion that sends one looking through patterns and fabric departments. Somehow, with the discovery of the right fabric, all these sources of inspiration come together – smocking designs, therefore, usually start with fabric.

## FABRIC

There is a wide range of fabrics available today which are of high quality and very suitable for smocking – unlike during the heyday of the traditional smock when a good solid linen was the best choice.

As the basic function of smocking is to hold fullness together in a decorative way, the most successful fabrics are supple and bouncy, with some body to hold the pleats formed by the smocking, and a good draping quality for the fullness. Many fashion fabrics are worth exploring to see what they offer on the use of a technique. To generate ideas, buy some small amounts of interesting fabrics and work some experimental samples.

Smocking can be used on many different weights of fabric, from heavy wool barathea to the finest crepe de chine. The matt surface of corduroy, velvet or wool challis will form a shadowed background to a silky thread, and fabrics like shot silks or taffeta, which catch the light, will show a color change when released in folds.

The type and weight of fabric should be suited to the garment, as well as the relative transparency and the regularity of the weave. For example, is there a check, stripe or dot which could be used to assist even rows of gathering? Will the smocking add a texture to the fabric, or could the smocking pattern and threads alter the coloring?

The few fabrics to avoid are the ones which are very pliable or stretchy, and those with a stiff finish. Fabrics which crease easily are not suitable as it is not possible to press smocked areas; and some crepons and other weaves form their own folds and do not lie happily in folds formed by smocking.

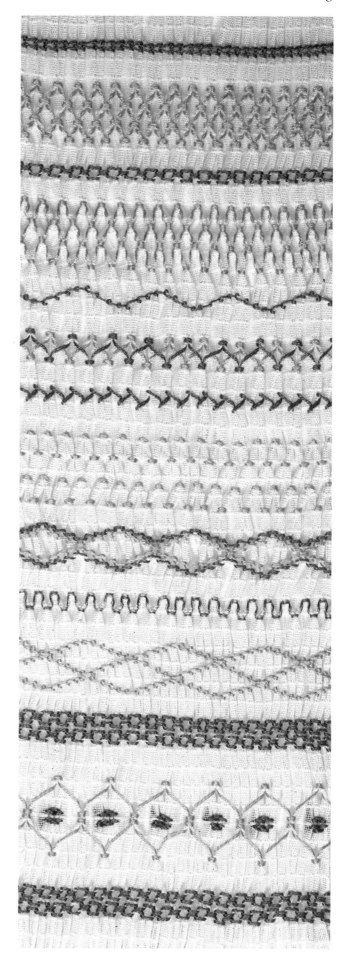

1.  *Double stem or Mockchain*

2.  *Surface Honeycomb*

3.  *Double Cable*

4.  *Vandyke or Honeycomb*

5.  *Feather*

6.  *Crossed diamond*

7.  *Herringbone*

8.  *Honeycomb or Spot Honeycomb*

9.  *Trellis or Close Wave*

10. *Vandyke or Honeycomb (twotone)*

11. *Feather trellis*

12. *Double Cable*

13. *Spaced Diamond (Cable between)*

14. *Double Cable*

## PLACING THE SMOCKED AREAS

The shape and placing of smocking should enhance the style lines and bring out the main features of the dress, becoming in the process an integral and balanced part of the whole design and not just an isolated area.

Look for places where fullness needs to be drawn in and then flow out, such as sleeves or skirts. Fullness can fall from smocking placed as shown in the fashion sketches opposite:

1. All around a close-fitting neckband. High necks can be smocked all round with little rouleau loops and buttons fastening the rows, allowing the fullness to fall to the hem of a loose raglan-cut blouse or evening coat. The smocked neck section is cut in one piece with each extended bodice and sleeve section.

2. On a frill.

3. Around a wide neck-line, just sitting on the shoulders.

4. Inserted in various types and depths of yokes placed across the shoulders. If the yokes have a straight edge it is easier to work the smocking.

5. Over the whole area which would have formed the yoke.

6. On the head of a sleeve. An area can be smocked and then set into the arm-hole.

7. On the top shoulder section of a raglan sleeve.

8. At the wrist edge of a sleeve – this can be seen on various sketches – the fullness can be drawn in by a narrow band of smocking with a frilled edge, or a wide band forming a cuff. The edge could be bound or set into a narrow cuff.

9. At the waist. Any garment which has sufficient fullness could be drawn in by a few lines of a simple smocking stitch which would fit the figure lightly.

10. On a wide hip band, which can be smocked down from the waistline and will act as a fitted hip yoke to a full skirt.

11. All over strapless tops, particularly a large-scale Honeycomb stitch. Horizontal or vertical rows of Cable stitch with spaces between to reveal the gathered fabric give an interesting effect rather like that of shirring.

12. On a halter-neck top. An evening gown in this style would be very attractive smocked with metallic threads or with added beads.

13. A whole garment such as a vest can be smocked to give an all-over texture, contrasting with the appearance of the flat fabric in the rest of the outfit.

## THE CUT

The best drape is achieved from gathers hanging with the straight grain, or warpwise, and this arises naturally from the fact that panels or rows of smocking are normally worked at right angles across the grain from selvage to selvage, the gathering following along the weft thread.

The finished piece of smocking is usually set into a band or straight yoke line, or is gathered to a neckline, waistline or cuff with a previously prepared frilled edge.

## CURVED EDGE

Smocking can be worked along a slightly curved edge which will be set into a curved yoke. Here the tubes will be slightly 'off grain' in places. The dots used to guide the gathering will have to be slashed and shaped out to the flat along the area to be smocked, as shown here and on page 15, before being marked in position.

Examples of this curved smocking are the crepe de chine dress with the narrow yoke, and the neck of the black coat. Note that on the patterns the edge is only slightly curved, and the effect of a rounder line is achieved by using a raglan type sleeve. The seams are worked first, joining the sleeves to the back and front sections, so achieving a flat surface and a continuous row of straight gathers for smocking.

If a greater curve were used, the gathers would become very distorted across the weave and the fullness would not hang well.

## CALCULATING THE AMOUNT OF FABRIC REQUIRED

The amount of fabric required for each smocked section varies for the following reasons:

**The thickness of the fabric.** A thicker fabric will take up more space, so slightly less will be required than for a finer weight used for the same style and with the same stitch.

**The scale of the smocking.** The space between the rows and the gathers can be varied to suit the fabric thickness. However this only makes a minimal difference to the amount of fabric required.

**The tension.** Smockers generally have their own tension and after a few experiments it is possible to know whether it is tighter or looser than normal. Try to keep it as even as possible.

**The choice of stitch.** This creates the most variation in the amount of fabric required. All smocking should remain with some stretch, and not be stretched to the utmost, so allow the full amount of width. Cable and Stem stitch and close rows of Wave stitch need three times the finished width, and Honeycomb stitches, including Vandyke stitch need just over twice the amount.

Honeycomb stitch allows the finished smocking to pull out more than other stitches, making the spaces which give the honeycomb effect – however too much fabric may leave the tubes too close together and the effect will be lost.

To calculate the amount of fabric required for smocking when used on a shaped part of a garment, such as a low neckline over the shoulders or a hip band from the waist, the measurement of the final released size of the smocking should be that of the largest circumference of that part of the body. Edges, such as the waistline or neckline, can be pulled in slightly to fit.

**Sample calculations** for a smocked area stretched out over a curve from waist to hips:

| | |
|---|---|
| Minimum waist size | 26in. (66cm) |
| Maximum 4in. (10cm) below waist | 32in. (82cm) |

A 4in. (10cm) band of smocking, therefore, must stretch to more than 32in. (82cm).

**Fabric required for loose stitch** such as Honeycomb will be twice 36in. (90cm), which is 72in. (180cm).

**Fabric required for tight stitch** such as Wave or Cable will be three times 36in. (90cm), which is 108in. (270cm).

**Loss of length.** Smocking always takes up a certain amount of length, depending on the stitch and the number of rows. For example, the all-over smocked vest on page 76 lost a quarter of its length in working. If it is very important to calculate this, the only sure way is to work a sample, otherwise always allow extra fabric lengthwise.

## GATHERING

Methods of transferring dot patterns to the fabric are described on pages 14–15. Smocking dot transfers are particularly useful when the rows follow a slightly curved edge, and the tissue can be slashed every inch or so until it lies flat on the curve.

Weaves and prints can be used as the basis of regular rows of gathering (though smocking based on these can only be worked along straight edges). Fine checks give good even gathers, and interesting color changes can be achieved by drawing light color to the surface of the smocking and leaving others in the background. Open weaves can be picked up by counted thread, and weaves with an integral spot form a built-in dot pattern, as long as the scale is suitable. Stripes are not as easy as checks or dots to use as a base.

Printed patterns must be regularly printed on the straight grain of the fabric to be of any use, and this should be checked first – prints are so often slightly off grain and can distort the smocking. The scale of the pattern and the density of print must be suitable for the type of smocking to be worked.

Regular flower motifs can be used by drawing them together on the right side with Spot Honeycomb stitch, so avoiding the tedious gathering stage – this is sometimes termed Direct Smocking. This type of smocking can also be worked on a new and popular fabric, which is a soft mock suede on a knit background with regular rows of tiny holes, just the right density for smocking.

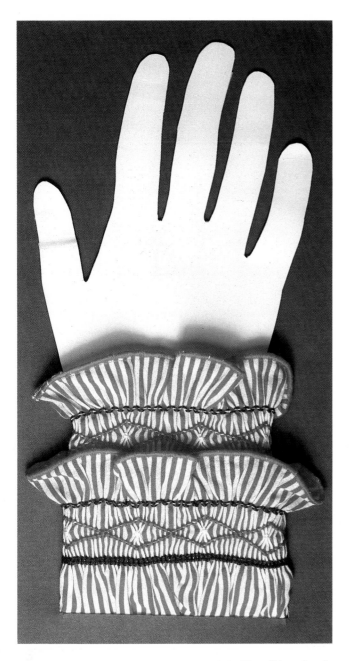

**Smocked cuff.** *By Chris Reid. A smocked double cuff in red and white striped cotton – the top row is Cable stitch, the middle is Trellis stitch and the bottom row is Outline and Stem stitches.*
*All three rows are worked in DMC Pearle No. 5. The edge of the cuff was satin-stitched by machine with ordinary sewing cotton.*

**Smocked cuff.** *By Ann Tranquillini. Flowered fabric smocked into a cuff, with rouleau loop fastening.*

# Direct smocking on punched-hole fabric

Take twice the required width of fabric, and use buttonhole twist or matching strong thread and a blunt-ended tapestry needle. Work from right to left on the right side of the fabric.

1. Secure end of thread. Pass the needle in and out of four holes in the same row.

2. Stitch twice more through the same holes, and pull the thread tight.

3. Pass the needle down the back to the next row.

4. Work the stitch through three holes, and then over again twice through four holes.

5. Pass the thread back up again to the level of the first stitch and continue.

6. This pattern can be worked on every other row.

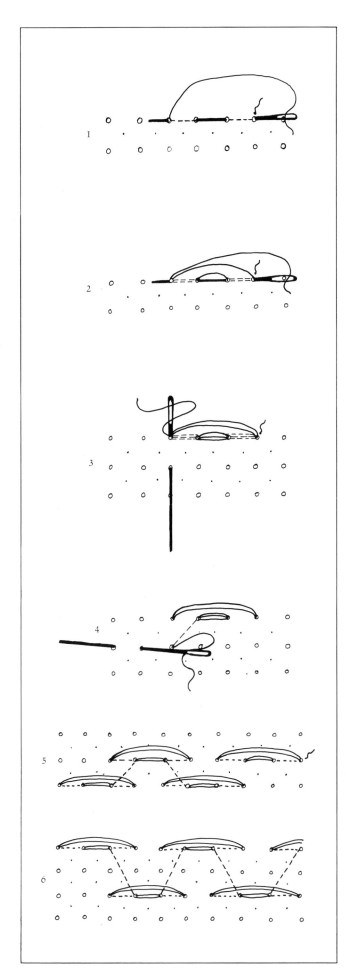

**Direct smocking on punched suede.** *By Ann Tranquillini. The neckline of a jumpsuit in punched suede smocked on the right side.*

# Vest and skirt

A floral print fabric in black with colored flowers was used for this two-piece – the print is used plain for the skirt, and is smocked all over for the vest, giving it a weight and texture and an effect of light and shade. The smocking is worked in Honeycomb stitch in a black thread, leaving the bright colors of the flowers peeping through.

The reverse effect could also be interesting – if a white background fabric were smocked in white thread, which would give a light haze over the smocked area.

**Size.** Size 10, the skirt measures 28in. (71cm) from waist to bottom of frilled hem.

**Pattern.** As graph. Scale up as shown on page 30.

**Fabric.** 3¾yds (3.40m) of 36in. (90cm) wide fabric. About 1yd (1m) of a soft crepe for lining. Piping cord.

**Elastic.** Black tape or ribbon for trimming skirt.

**Smocking dots.** Use a scale of not less than ⅜in. (10mm), depending on the printed pattern. Iron the dots on to the wrong side of the fabric. Some regular patterns may look better worked with Spot Honeycomb. Work a small sample to try out the effect.

**Smocked area.** The smocking is worked all over the vest – but first prepare the lower edge as a frill and sew on the ribbon trim.

## ORDER OF WORK

Lay out the pattern pieces on the fabric, and cut out with a seam allowance of ⅝in. (15mm) all round, except for the skirt seams which should be about 1in. (2.5cm). Prepare bias strips for piping and rouleaux. (The vest lining is cut to fit when the smocking is complete.)

### Vest

Stitch the back and front side seams together, but not the shoulders. Turn up the lower edge for a frill and press, and stitch into place just under the lowest line of dots for gathering. Stitch ribbon trim just above fold edge of frill on right side. Treat the frill edges of the shoulder straps the same way. Work the gathering in continuous rows from left center front to right center front on the wrong side, and the rows on the shoulder sections. Pull up the gathers.

Work Honeycomb stitch with three strands in the needle over the whole area. Start at the frill edge on the right side with the work upside down. Work Cable stitch across the shoulder strips.

**Vest and skirt.** *By Ann Tranquillini. A flowered cotton skirt with the same fabric used as a vest which has been smocked to enhance the color and texture.*

Remove all gathering threads. Pull smocking into shape, correcting the measurements, and allowing the smocking to remain shaped in towards the shoulders to fit the shoulder strip. Then set by steam as shown on page 17. Stitch shoulder seams by hand, stab-stitching between the folds of the first line of smocking of the shoulder section, which is laid over the shoulder line of the vest.

Make loop and toggle fastenings from prepared rouleaux and cover piping cord with bias strips. Stitch the prepared piping all round the edge of the vest to hold the shape (except frill edge). Stitch fastenings in place. (See page 120.) Cut a lining to fit and stitch in place.

## Skirt

Seam the four skirt panels. Face waist edge. Make a double row of stitching to form a casing for the elastic, and leave a frill at the top edge. Trim the top edge with ribbon. Insert elastic to fit waist. Turn up hem.

Join the frill sections together. Hem edges and trim with ribbon. Gather 1in. (2.5cm) below top edge, and set on to the skirt at the hem line.

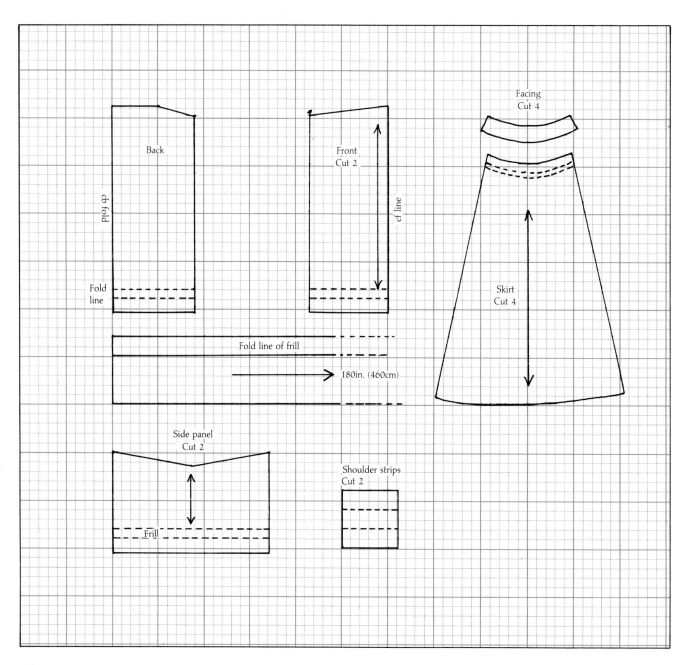

**Chart for vest and skirt.** *By Ann Tranquillini.*

# Smocked coat

This design can be made in many different weights of fabric for summer or for winter. The shape can also be adapted for blouses, dresses, jackets etc.

The coat illustrated opposite is made in a very thick black barathea – which is not a fabric that would normally be considered suitable for smocking. After experimentation, however, and trying out some samples, it was found that Spot Honeycomb stitch formed a design of simple elegance that held the heavy pleats firmly in place.

**Size.** To fit sizes 8 to 10. The measurement from neckline to hem is 45in. (114cm), and from shoulder point to wrist is 22in. (56cm).

**Pattern.** As graph, to the scale of one square = 1sq.in. (2.5sq.cm). Extra length is allowed front and back of ½in. (1.25cm) per three rows of smocking and over 3in. (8cm) to the sleeves, to allow them to hang above the cuff smocking. The coat neckline has 1in. (2.5cm) added to stand above the natural neckline.

**Fabric.** 2¾yds (2.50m) of black barathea 54in. (137cm) wide. An equal amount of lining. Satin for piping edges. Interlining for neckline and center front fastening.

**Smocking dots.** A scale of ½in. (1.25cm) apart was needed, but as a transfer in this size was not available a quarter-inch size was used and every other dot was picked up.

**Smocked area.** The yoke line should sit on the shoulders with the smocking lying over the shoulder into the sleeve head, the total circuit – front, back and sleeve – should measure more than twice the yoke edge.

## ORDER OF WORK

1. Scale up the pattern as described on page 30. Lay pattern pieces on fabric and cut out with preferred seam allowance, i.e., 1in. (2.5cm) side seam, and ⅝in. (1.5cm) elsewhere.
2. Slash and shape dot transfer to fit circular yoke, and cut out sections for the cuff area.
3. Iron on dots (see pages 16–17 for dots over seams).
4. Join sleeve seams on front and back.
5. Work gathers on all sections.
6. Draw up yoke gathers, smaller than yoke, ready for smocking.
7. Work the smocking around the yoke in embroidery floss matching the fabric, using Spot Honeycomb stitch, and working from right to left. On the last row of the yoke, skip every other group of gathers to leave a pointed edge.
8. Complete sleeve and side coat seams.
9. Draw up sleeve gathers.
10. Smock round cuff edge continuously over the seam.
11. Remove gathering threads, except for the top row of the yoke and the lowest row of the cuff.
12. Steam the smocking into shape to fit the yoke, as described on page 16.
13. Pipe the edge of the yoke (as on page 72) with satin before setting it on to the smocking and gathered lining.

Join front and back yoke facing together, and shoulder seam. Baste yoke. Baste interlining to yoke around neck edge and center front fold line.

14. Face and line the yoke to cover all the raw edges – this can be bulky, but careful layering and trimming should minimize it.

15. Bind the sleeve edges over the gathers and the lining with a bias strip of coat fabric to fit the wrist.
16. Make up the rest of the coat.

**Chart for smocked coat.** *By Ann Tranquillini.*

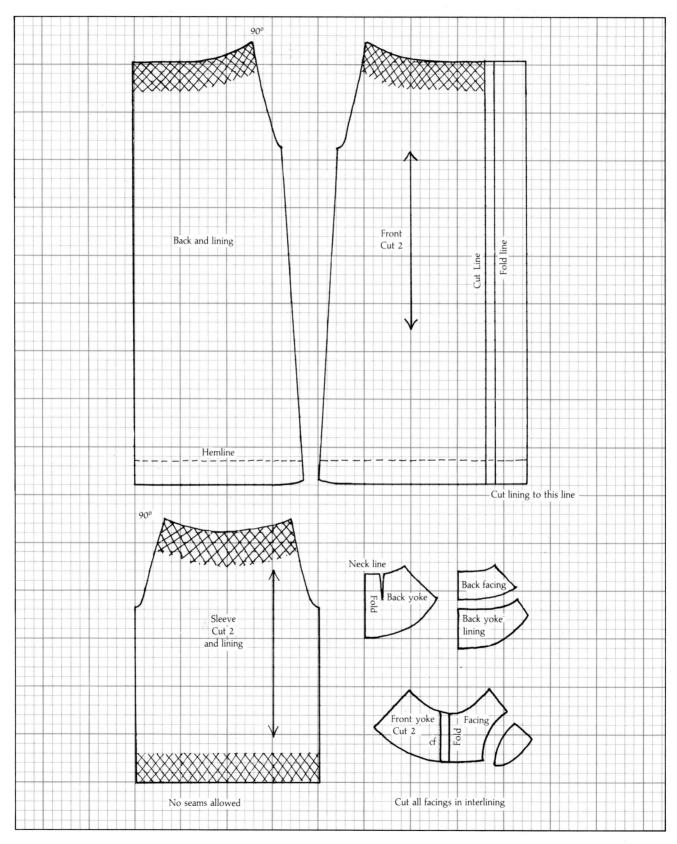

**Smocked coat.** *By Ann Tranquillini. A simple and timelessly elegant coat with a round yoke. Made of black barathea, the coat hangs in thick folds from a curved yoke, which is piped in black satin.*

*The smocking is done in Spot Honeycomb, a stitch which makes deep shadows and suits the weight of the fabric and the restraint of the design.*

**Silk wedding dress.** *By Dorothy Reglar. The front and back and a small section of the upper sleeves of this cream silk wedding dress are smocked and embroidered in cream silk buttonhole twist. The stitches used are Outline, Wave, Honeycomb and Surface Honeycomb.*

*The front neck opening is incorporated in the front smocked panel, which fastens with small pearl buttons and worked loops and rouleau ties with knotted ends. The surface embroidery on the yoke and collar is Feather stitch, which is also used to emphasize the seams.*

**Wool wedding dress.** *By Dorothy Reglar. The front and back panels of this white wool wedding dress are smocked in cream and white woollen threads. The stitches used are Outline, Cable and Trellis. The top of the sleeves and the wrists are also smocked. The cuffs, yoke and sleeve seams are decorated with Feather stitch. The neckline and cuffs are fastened with ties.*

# Crepe de chine dress

The beautiful fabric of this dress falls in perfect folds from a smocked neckline, and smocking gathers each sleeve into a soft cuff. The pattern is very similar to that of the black coat, and the smocking is worked in Honeycomb stitch.

**Size.** Sizes 8 to 10. The length from neck to hem is 45in. (114cm), and from shoulder to wrist is 22in. (56cm).

**Pattern.** As graph, to the scale of one square = 1sq.in. (2.5sq.cm). Scale up the pattern as described on page 30.

**Fabric.** 3½yds (3.25m) of pure silk crepe de chine in ivory, 45in. (114cm) wide. Satin for rouleau ties at neck and cuffs.

**Smocking dots.** A scale of ¼in. (6mm) was used. A transfer can be ironed onto the wrong side, but if the dots show through and it is a non-washable fabric (as some crepe de chines are), then the tissue-basting method of transferring dots (pages 16–17) should be used.

**Smocked area.** The smocking is gathered into a narrow yoke around the boat neckline, and finishes in points at the lower edge. The sleeve smocking at the lower edge is gathered into a binding.

## ORDER OF WORK

1. Lay out pattern pieces on the fabric. Cut out with a seam allowance of ⅝in. (1.5cm).
2. Slash and shape dot transfer or tissue to fit the circular yoke, and cut out sections for the cuffs. Transfer dots to fabric. See page 16 for joining dots at seams.
3. Join sleeve seams to front and back.
4. Pull up gathers around neckline.
5. Mark a small gap at the center front for an opening. Work three complete rows of Honeycomb stitch in silk or cotton embroidery thread all around, starting at the left of the marked gap and finishing at the right.
6. Work the pointed edge as follows: start at the center back and work the stitch on the three central groups; turn the work the other way up and stitch two groups in the opposite direction; turn the work again and stitch the last group, forming a point. Thread the needle back through the folds to work the next point, continuing round to the center front. Start again at the center back, and work in the opposite direction to complete the other half of the yoke. Try to even up these points at the center front opening – matching right and left sides, and incorporating an extra fold in the opening if necessary.
7. Join dress side seams, and sleeve under-arm seams.
8. Pull up gathers right around sleeves.
9. Smock three rows of Honeycomb stitch around the sleeves and work points as at yoke edge. Start at center of sleeve and work towards seam.
10. Remove gathers except for top row of yoke and lowest row of cuff.

**Crepe de chine dress.** *By Ann Tranquillini. The silk fabric falls in soft folds from a round yoke, fastened in front with a rouleau box.*

11. If loops are preferred to rouleaux for fastening, add these now, or bind the smocked lower edge of the sleeves with a bias strip of satin. If preferred, add loops and buttons.

12. Bind the small opening at center front of bodice with a bias strip of satin.

13. Bind the top edge of the double yoke with a satin bias strip, which can be extended into a rouleau tie. On the lower edge of the yoke machine one side of the satin binding in place around the upper layer only, turn the binding over and press down, and then set this lower edge onto the smocking. Neaten the inner side of the yoke on the wrong side, covering the gathers with the yoke lining.

14. Turn up hem.

**Chart for crepe de chine dress.** *By Ann Tranquillini.*

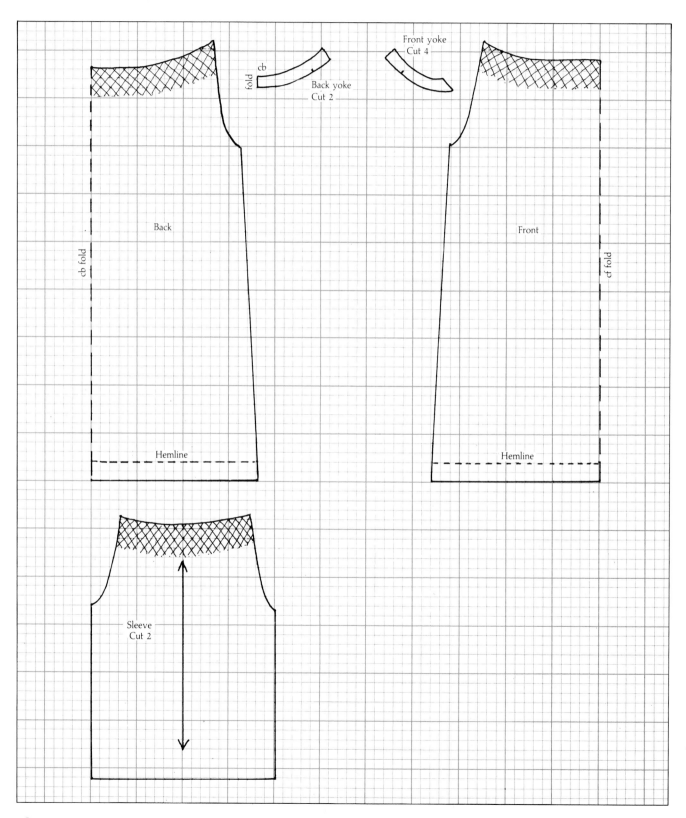

# Frilled collar

The deep band of smocking on this collar frill is worked on a drip-dry polyester fabric, in the colors of the printed pattern on the fabric of the cotton dress. This kind of collar can be detachable, and is best made in a crease-resistant fabric to remain crisp in wear.

**Fabric.** Two widths of 45in. (115cm) fabric were joined, forming a strip 90in. × 10in. (230cm × 25cm). A narrow cross stitch hem was worked along one long edge.

**Thread.** Three strands of embroidery floss.

**Smocking dots.** The fabric had an even dot in the weave which was used as a guide for the gathers – otherwise use a ¼in. (6mm) smocking dot transfer, ironed onto the back.

**Frilled collar.** *By Pat Steward.*

**Smocked area.** There are ten rows of gathers along the length of the fabric ⅜in. (10mm) apart, and a ½in. (12mm) hem along the short ends, secured at the neck edge to the back zip of the dress.

**Smocking.** Draw up the first row of gathers to fit the neck. Stitches used are Cable, Diamond, Wave and Double Vandyke, finishing in points on the last row. The neck edge is bound to the neck of the dress with a bias strip.

*Every kind of smocking*

**Muslin blouse.** *By Dorothy Reglar. White dotted Swiss blouse, smocked around the neck with green silk thread. The neckline is edged with a narrow band of slotted crocheting which is drawn up with a silk cord.*

*The blouse consists of one piece of fabric folded over, as shown in the diagram. The cut edges should be neatened by turning under a ¼in. (6mm) hem onto the right side – this gives a strong white edge. Oversew the crochet edging to the neck and sleeve hems in matching thread. The smocking stitches around the neckline are Outline, Surface Honeycomb, Double Cable and Wave stitch.*

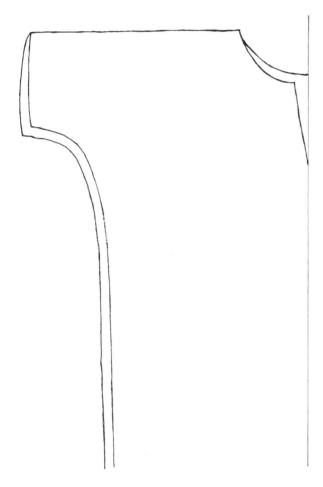

**Silk blouse.** *By Dorothy Reglar. This cream silk blouse is smocked at neck and elbow with self-colored silk buttonhole twist. The smocking stitches used are Outline, Wave, Double Cable and Surface Honeycomb. Three rows of Surface Honeycomb give elasticity on the elbow.*

*Sew in and neaten the raglan sleeves before gathering and smocking. Work embroidery over the dart along the shoulder into the neck. Edge the sleeves and hem with cream lace.*

# Waisted dress

This dress is made in a pretty shade of gold wool and has a panel of smocking down the front, edged with lines of Feather stitch and embroidered motifs. The back is held in with deep vertical pleats decorated with lines of Feather stitching. Four embroidered buttons hold the waist sash. The sleeves have a small smocked area on the shoulder and a larger area just above the cuff, which is fastened with another embroidered button. The neckline, cuffs and hem are embroidered with Double Feather stitching.

**Size.** Two pattern sizes are given; sizes 8 to 10 and 12 to 14. The dress measures about 16in. (41cm) from neck to waist (lowest line of smocking), and 43in. (110cm) from neck to hem. The waistline can be adjusted to fit by altering the depth of the smocked section.

**Fabric.** 3⅓yds (3m) of wool challis 45in. (114cm) wide.

**Threads.** Thick embroidery silk was used for the smocking, in shades of pale gold, green and terracotta. Pearl cotton or three strands of embroidery floss could be substituted.

**Pattern.** This pattern is based on the traditional rectangular smock shapes. The chart is not drawn to scale but shows the cutting layout. The seam allowance on all pieces is ⅜in. (1cm). The measurements for the separate pieces are as follows:

|  | Sizes 8–10 | Sizes 12–14 |
|---|---|---|
| Back and Front | 36in. × 45in. (90cm × 114cm) | 36½in. × 45in. (91.3cm × 114cm) |
| Sleeves | 17¾in. × 20in. (45cm × 51cm) | 18¼in. × 20in.) (46.5cm × 51cm) |
| Gussets | 4¾in. square (12cm square) | |
| Yokes (2 used as facings) | 6¼in. × 9in. (16cm × 23cm) | 6¾in. × 9in. (17.3cm × 23cm) |
| Ties (4) | 2in. × 30in. (5cm × 76cm) | |

**Smocking dots.** Use a scale ¼in. (6cm) apart – both rows and dots. Iron transfer dots onto the wrong side of the fabric.

**Smocked area.** The center front panel consists of 45 rows of 95 dots. Center the dot transfer, with the top row of dots level with the seam allowance.

The sleeve cuff consists of 11 rows of 51 dots, and the sleeve top of 11 rows of 19 dots. Both should be centered, with the appropriate row of dots level with the seam allowance.

**Waisted dress with smocked panel.** *By Pat Steward. This dress has a square neck with a deep smocked panel extending to the waistline, edged with embroidery. The sleeves are raglan, and the side panels are embroidered.*

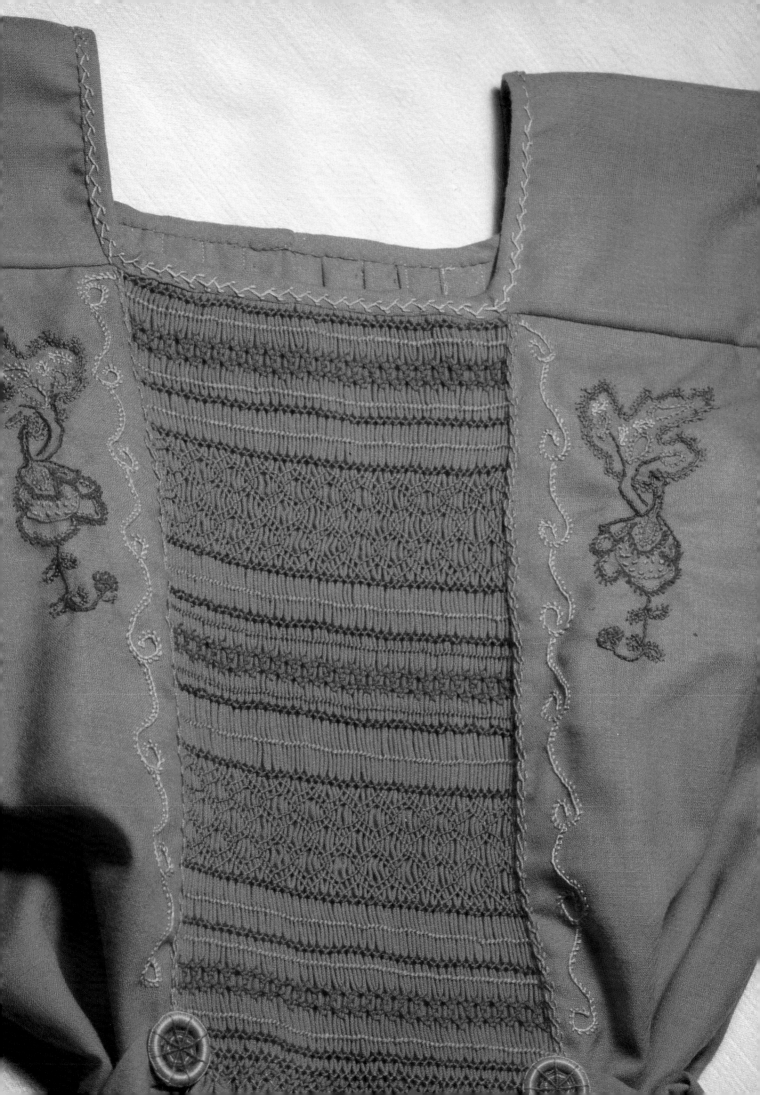

**SMOCKING**

**Front panel.** There are 45 rows of gathers. Leave the first line and start at the second.

ROW 1. Cable stitch. Starting thread above needle.

ROW 2. Outline stitch. Thread above needle.

ROWS 3 to 5. Feathered Diamond.

ROW 6. Outline stitch. Thread below needle.

ROW 7. Cable stitch. Starting thread below needle.

ROW 8. Space.

ROW 9. Outline stitch. Thread above needle.

ROW 10. Cable stitch. Starting thread above needle.

ROWS between cables on 10 to 14. Trellis stitch, 5 up and 5 down in double rows.

ROW 14. Cable stitch. Starting thread below needle.

ROW 15. Outline stitch. Thread below needle.

ROW 16. Space.

ROWS 17 to 31. Repeat above pattern.

ROWS 32 to 34. Repeat Feathered Diamond.

ROW 35. Outline stitch.

ROW 36. Cable stitch.

Complete with enough rows of parallel half-diamonds to make suitable bodice length to waist. Sew a piece of elastic across the bottom of the smocked panel on the inside.

**Sleeve top** – use pattern rows 1 to 12.

**Sleeve cuff** – use pattern rows 10 to 15. Omit last Cable.

Set smocking (see page 16) and remove all gathering threads except the top row of the skirt.

**EMBROIDERY**

1. Work one row of Single Feather stitch down each side of all panels.
2. Work scrolls in Single Feather.
3. A motif can be embroidered each side of the smocking, in the manner of traditional smocks.
4. Back of smock. Mark the center, and pleat center panel to equal the measurement of the smocked front. Three or four tucks will be needed on each side of the center. Stitch �5⁄16in. (8mm) from the edge, and work a line of Feather stitching down each tuck by the inner side of the machined line. Sew a piece of straight binding across the bottom of the tucks on the inside.

**TO MAKE UP**

**Yokes.** With right sides together, baste yokes lengthwise between back and front. Baste yoke facing inside (right side facing to wrong side of dress) and stitch through. Baste neck and arm-hole edges together. Bind neck edge all round with bias strip.

**Sleeves.** Sew one side gusset to sleeve edge at top, fold sleeve in half, pin together with gusset folded diagonally, and stitch seam, leaving a wrist end opening of 3in. (8cm). Hem the opening.

**Cuffs.** Fold in half, right sides together (interlining may be basted to one half). Stitch across the short ends. Turn right side out, and stitch on edge of cuff to sleeve, leaving an extension of 1in. (2.5cm) on the outside edge of the opening. Turn under the other edge of the cuff and slip-stitch in place. Work a line of Feather stitching around the edge of the cuff.

Sew the sleeves to the dress, matching the center of the top edge of the smocked panel to the center of the yokes.

Sew side seams.

**Ties.** Make a tie by folding it in half, right sides together, and stitch, leaving one short end open. Turn out and close other end. Embroider a motif on the ends. Stitch ties to the corners of the front panel over elastic ends, and to the back panel over the straight binding ends.

Work buttonholes in cuffs.

Make six traditional buttons (see page 121) and sew on to cuffs and over ties.

**Hem.** Embroider a line of Feather stitching above the turn-up line, or above the hemline, then turn up the hem to cover the back of the embroidery.

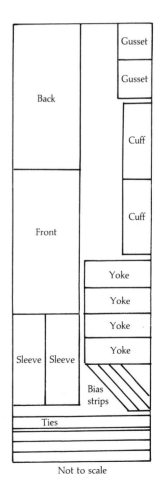

Not to scale

**Chart for waisted dress.** *By Pat Steward.*

# CHAPTER 5

# *Experimental smocking*

# Experimental smocking

The elasticity of the smocking technique, together with its textural and decorative qualities, makes it highly suitable for creative and experimental work. The long tubes formed by the gathers are also traditionally known as 'reeds', a word which evokes willowy linear forms and indicates ways in which this previously disciplined work may be adapted to a free approach.

## Equipment

Much of the basic equipment described in previous sections of this book is also appropriate to this aspect of smocking. A frame may be necessary when applying pieces of freely smocked fabric to a background.

## Transfer of dots

Dots may be drawn on the reverse of the fabric with a hard sharp pencil or a fabric pen. This has the advantage of flexibility when marking out work for irregular effects.

## Fabrics

Smocking works particularly well on plain and pliable fabrics such as soft cottons and wools, but less obvious choices can often be used to dramatic effect – try fabrics such as glove leather, suede, corded velvet, linen scrim and even some kinds of vinyl.

## Dyes

Fabric can be dyed before or after smocking, using fabric dyes, inks or even car sprays. Pieces of fabric pre-dyed in gradations of color can look very attractive, and paint can be sprayed or sponged onto certain areas either before or after smocking. Dye can be applied to the surface of the smocking before the gathering stitches have been removed, lightly stroked on with a sponge, and when the gathering threads are removed the resulting piece will have a two-tone effect which exaggerates the depth of the gathers. As there is no problem of washability where these pieces are concerned, the field for experiment is wide.

## Surface smocking

Surface smocking on the front of the gathers is normally worked in straight rows with even tension, using a suitable thread for the fabric. By altering the tension or the direction of stitches, or the size of the gathers or the threads, exciting effects may be achieved. Try working some small samples to explore the possibilities with your chosen fabric and threads before embarking on a major piece of work.

For a first sample, mark out the guide dots on the reverse of the fabric – the scale of the dots will depend on the scale of the finished piece, but ½in. (1.5cm) apart is a reasonable scale with which to start. Baste the rows and draw them up in the usual way. Work Stem stitch on the front of the gathers in an irregular manner, varying the closeness and direction of the stitches, then work the smocking trying to add contrasts to the stitched and unmarked areas (Fig. 1). Withdraw the gathering threads.

Mount background fabric on an embroidery frame. Fabric may be the same as the smocked piece, or a contrast. Lay the smocking in place and with the aid of dressmaking pins manipulate the fabric until the desired effect has been achieved. This may take several re-arrangements. Some areas may be squeezed together and others pulled apart to reveal interesting and contrasting shapes. When the result is satisfactory, stitch the applied piece to the background using a matching sewing thread (Fig. 2).

Further surface embroidery may now be worked as required, perhaps some stitches such as French knots, Loops or Bullion knots. Running stitches or seeding will enhance the linear quality of the smocking. The addition of textured yarns or fine ribbons will contribute to the surface interest. Smocking stitches may also be used in this way – Spot Honeycomb stitch used irregularly works particularly well with cellular subjects such as tree bark and plant forms, as well as in a purely abstract manner (Fig. 2).

## Reverse smocking

In this technique the smocking stitches are worked on the reverse of the gathers, leaving the front totally clear for further decoration. Mark out the guide dots on the reverse of the fabric as usual, draw up the gathers, and work smocking stitches on the reverse side of the fabric.

You will now be faced with a flexible piece of fabric which is both pleasing to handle and full of possibilities for development. Gentle manipulation will reveal subtle and interesting patterns which will suggest ways of incorporating the piece into an embroidery design (Fig. 3).

The embroidery on page 101 was evolved in this way. It is an interpretation of a waterfall on a cliff face, in which several pieces of reverse smocking have been applied to the calico background. In addition some areas have been padded and others embroidered, and the waterfall itself consists of applied fragments of frayed fabrics.

**Cornfield with daisies.** *By Sheila Shaw. The pre-dyed fabric was worked in reverse smocking and applied to a background, and then surface stitching was added. The wheat ears are made of Bullion knots and Straight stitches, and the daisy petals are tiny strips of fabric.*

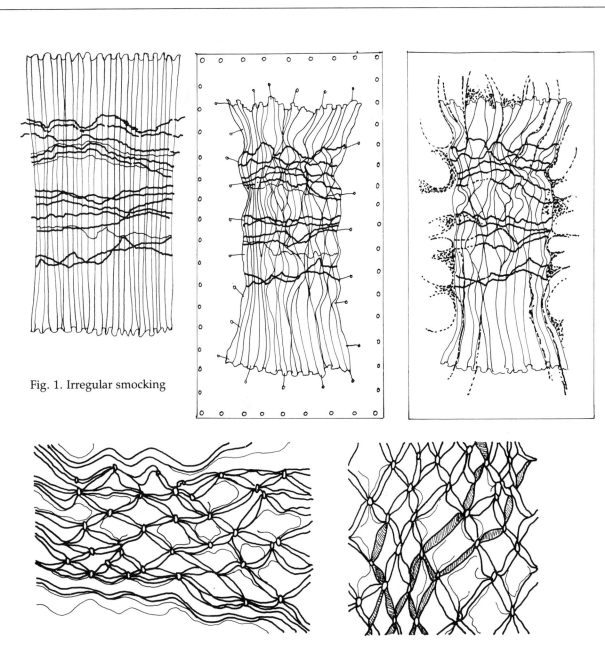

Fig. 1. Irregular smocking

Fig. 2. Irregular smocking with 'hidden' Honeycomb stitch

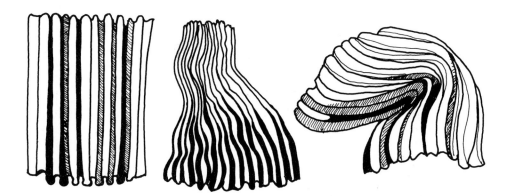

Fig. 3. Fabric gathered by reverse smocking

# *Three-dimensional design*

## Soft sculpture

Smocking can easily be manipulated into unusual shapes, making it a very suitable technique for three-dimensional work. Hold a piece of smocked fabric in your hands, and twist and turn it to see what forms it may suggest – shells, perhaps, or some other natural form. The fish above was manipulated into shape, stuffed and then embroidered.

It is also possible to start with a basic three-dimensional shape and add one or more pieces of smocking. Pin the piece onto the shape, and when the desired effect is reached, stitch it in place (Fig. 4).

**Three-dimensional fish.** *By Marie Zambra. The body was made in sections with sides smocked in variations of Honeycomb stitch, and stuffed with kapok. The fins were made of a double layer of fabric, machine-quilted and edged in Satin stitch.*

Fig. 4. Three-dimensional smocking

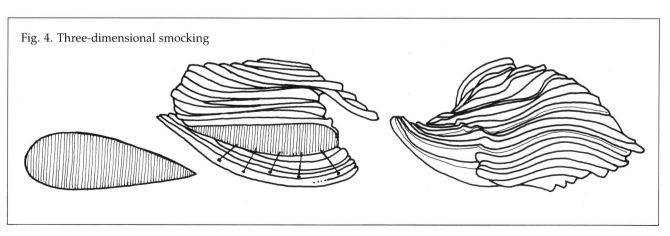

# Large-scale smocking

This can be very dramatic, and as it is not a very suitable project for small samples some idea of the final effect may be gained by using folding and stapling. Fold non-woven fabric or soft strong paper into pleats of the required depth, and using a tiny hand stapler, staple the folds together to simulate Honeycomb stitch (Fig. 5). In this way much experimentation may be carried out quickly. Dyes can also be used in various ways – spraying from different angles will throw interesting shadow effects onto the smocking. When a satisfactory balance is achieved, the design may be translated with confidence into fabrics and threads.

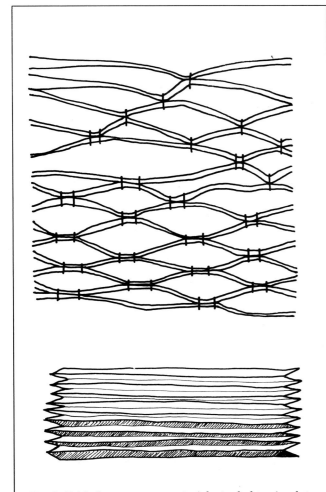

Fig. 5. Folded non-woven material, stapled to simulate smocking

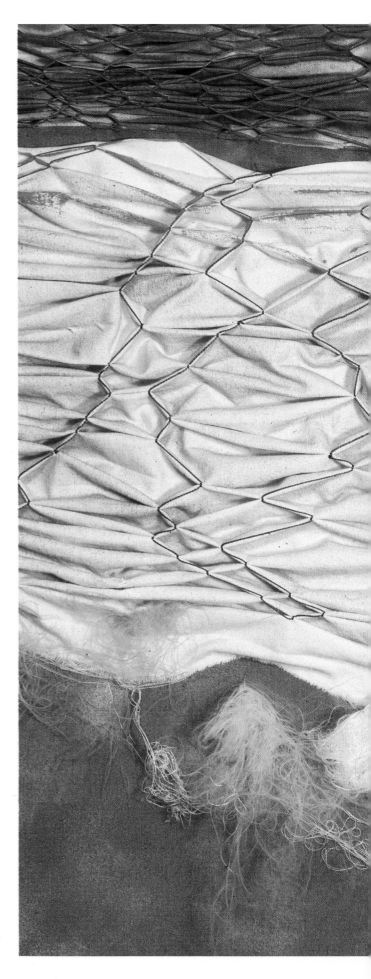

**Seascape.** *By Sue Atkinson. The panel measures 44in. × 27in. (112cm × 69cm). Three lengths of fabric were folded and spray-dyed before being randomly smocked with Honeycomb stitch. They were then mounted on fabric stretched on the frame, and the 'foam' at the edge of the waves was added.*

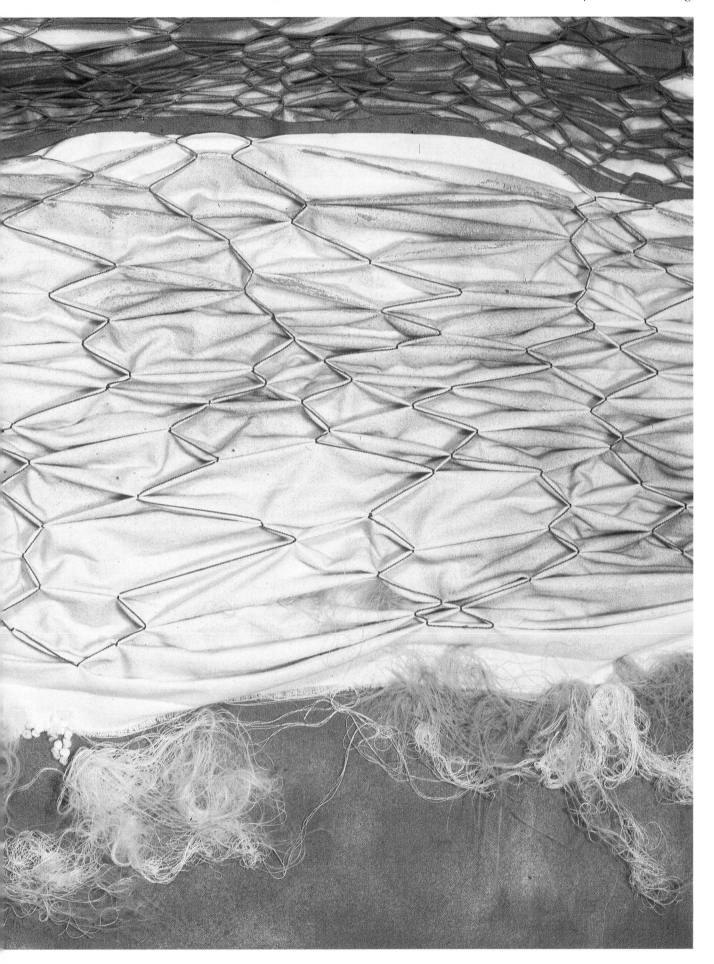

# Design ideas

## Design ideas

The simple starting points described may suggest ideas for further experimental work. There are numerous ways in which this technique may be developed. Fig. 6 shows three pieces of fabric applied to a background which, with the addition of regular Honeycomb smocking, could be used to interpret a landscape seen through the wire mesh of a fence.

Ridges or pleats can be stitched into the fabric as in Fig. 11, and used as smocking guides for a more formal effect (Fig. 7).

**Waterfall.** *By Georgina Rees. The rocks were worked in reverse smocking on dyed calico and then applied in sections to a calico background. Some areas were sprayed after the pieces were assembled. The waterfall was made from wisps of frayed fabrics.*

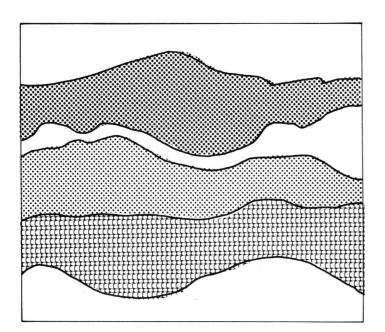
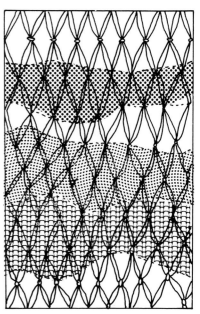

Fig. 6. Applied shapes with a smocked grid

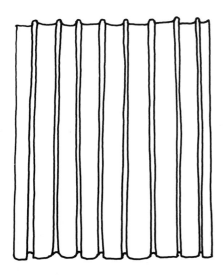
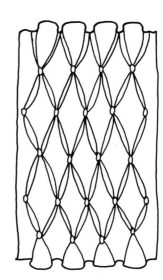

Fig. 7. Pleats as a basis for smocking

Several smocked pieces can be built up into a panel, as in the sweetcorn sample shown in Fig. 8. The central cob is worked first in random Honeycomb stitch, and the leaves on either side worked in reverse smocking and applied to produce a linear effect. The fronds at the top can be wools or frayed fabric.

The addition of threads, ribbons or beads to the surface of the smocking can result in an infinite variety of patterns and textures, such as those in Fig. 9.

The use of wire will give smocking an open structure. Insert florist's or electrical wire (thickness of the wire will depend on the scale of the work) into a number of finished rouleaux (see page 119), and oversew the ends. When sufficient pieces have been assembled, smock them together with Honeycomb stitch and a firm thread. Pull the structure gently into shape and add any further stitchery. Fig. 10 shows the stages involved in a design suggesting a trellis with flowers.

As with most embroidery, the secret of a successful piece of work lies in the selection of a suitable fabric and thread and a

**Smocked poppies.** *By Sheila Sturrock. The poppies are made from waterproof nylon. Four rows of smocking dots in the center of the fabric were worked in black embroidery floss, and the petals were cut to shape when the smocking was completed.*

source of design which enhances the technique to be used. Smocking is a linear technique with interesting depths, holes and ridges. Inspiration for design can be found throughout the natural world, or in man-made patterns, architecture and sculpture.

Simple landscapes, seascapes, or a ripple pattern on a beach all provide material for starting points – but beware of too literal an interpretation. Use the source as an initial inspiration, and allow the unique quality of smocking to be expressed in the finished design.

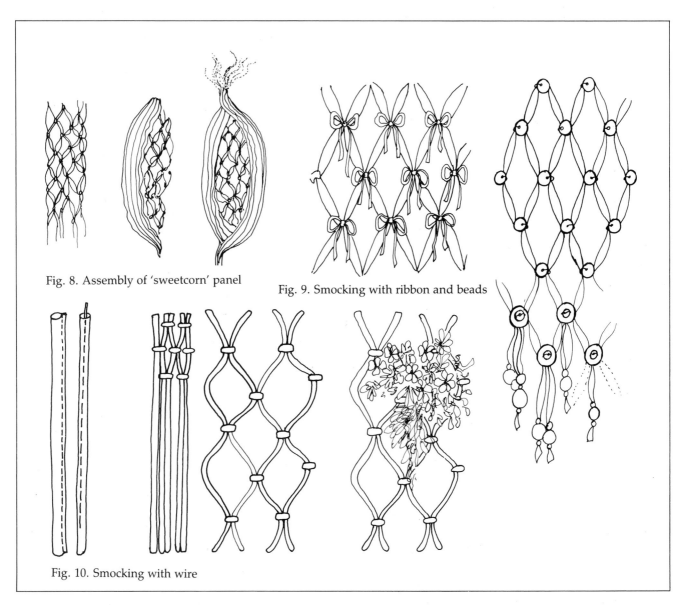

Fig. 8. Assembly of 'sweetcorn' panel

Fig. 9. Smocking with ribbon and beads

Fig. 10. Smocking with wire

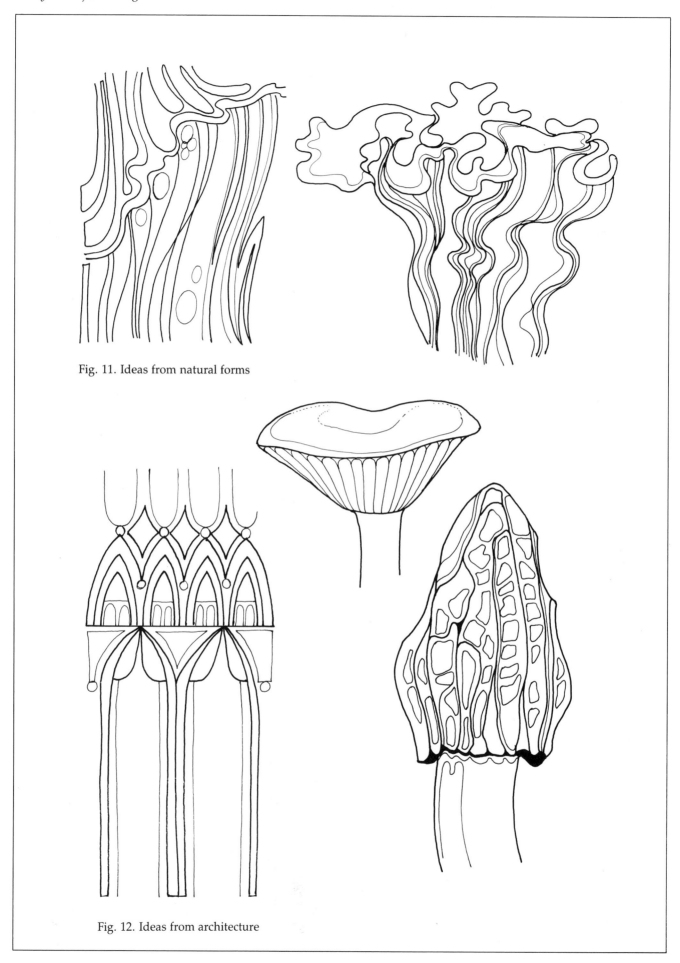

Fig. 11. Ideas from natural forms

Fig. 12. Ideas from architecture

# CHAPTER 6

# *Different kinds of smocking*

# Smocking with beading

Beading will add highlights to smocking, and it is particularly easy to apply beads to Honeycomb smocking, as there are two stitches holding each pair of tubes and the beads are thus sewn on securely. Make sure on any other pattern that each bead is held with two stitches.

Choose beads that will accord with the scale of the smocking and the weight of the fabric. Use sewing silk in a beading needle (or one fine enough to pass through the beads).

With Honeycomb stitch you can sew on the beads at the same time as working the smocking. Pass the needle through a bead each time you take a stitch, so that each bead is held on with two stitches.

Tiny bead motifs, like the ones on the collar above, can be worked before the garment is made up, and hand-made buttons such as the Dorset Birdseye (see page 121) can incorporate matching beads.

**Silk blouse with a beaded neckline.** *By Isabella Crocker. A deep band of Honeycomb smocking around the neckline ends in diamond points, and pearls and beads are sewn to the smocking stitches. The buttons down the back are rings covered with silk buttonholing, centered with a bead.*

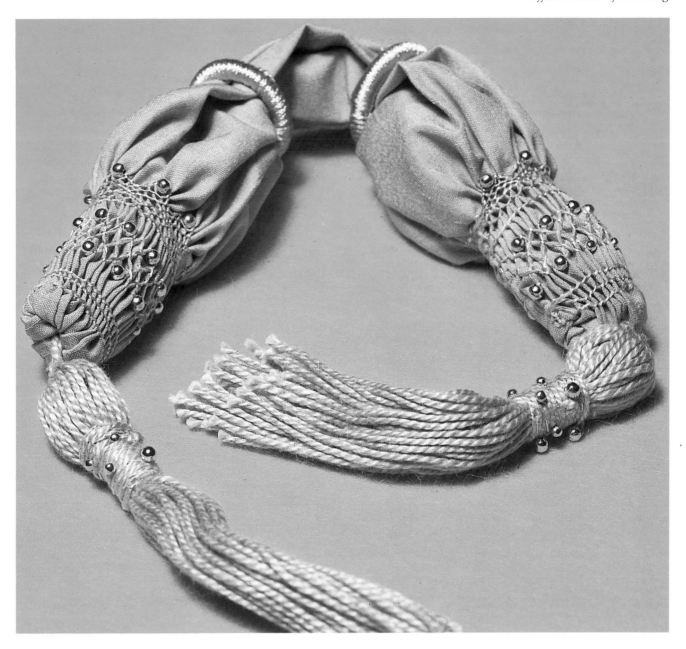

# *Miser's purse*

This is based upon the very ornate purses worn tucked over the belt in the sixteenth century. These were often worked in metal threads and tasselled – the same sort of purse was reproduced in the eighteenth and nineteenth centuries in beadwork and netting.

A rectangular piece of polyester silk, measuring approximately 9in. × 14in. (23cm × 35cm) was used. Rows of transfer dots were ironed on, 1in. (2.5cm) in from each narrow end. The smocking was worked in grey and lavender silk, variegated embroidery floss and silver thread. The silvered metal beads were sewn into the smocking as it was worked.

When finished, the fabric was folded lengthways, right sides together, and the seam on the long side was stitched

**Miser's purse.** *By Sheila Markham.*

down, leaving a central opening of about 4in. (10cm), which was hemmed. The seam was neatened. The smocked ends were gathered tightly one half-inch (about 1cm) above the top line of the smocking, and securely finished off. The purse was then turned right side out.

The tassels were made of thick grey cotton, and metal beads were applied to the finished wrappings before the tassels were sewn to the ends of the purse. The closure rings were wrapped in silver thread.

# Smocking with appliqué

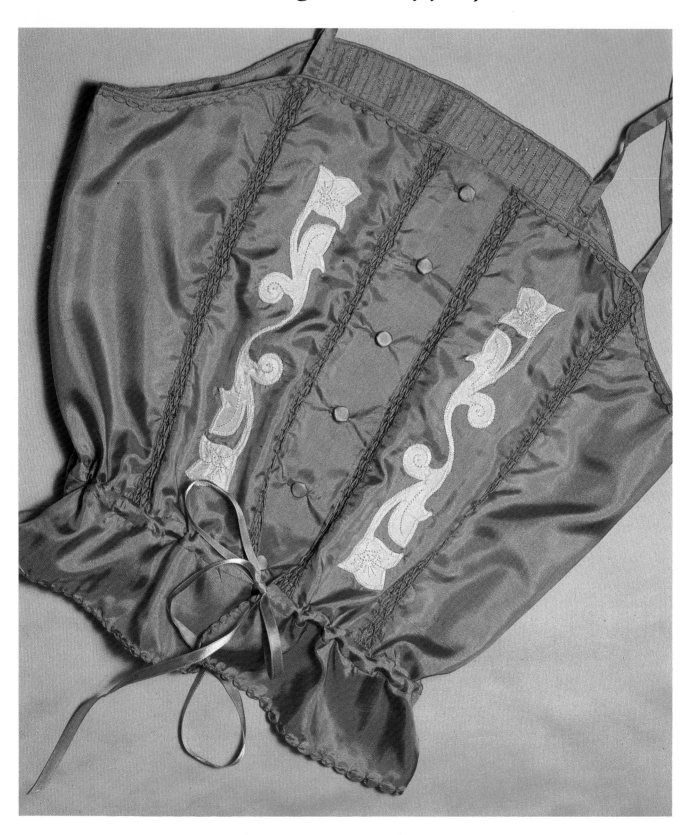

**Camisole.** *By Sheila Sturrock. Made of pure silk with appliqué in contrasting silk, smocked and pintucked in fine silk thread.*

**Wool crepe dress.** *By Dorothy Reglar. This dress is decorated with stitching in colored threads and leather appliqué. The yoke and sleeve bands were worked before the dress section was set on. The front fastens with a hand-made cord.*

# Smocking with embroidery

Honeycomb smocking gathers in the fabric across the handles of this workbag, and the fullness above it is pleated and stitched down over the bar. The main part of the bag is decorated with a pattern of eyelet holes.

To make a similar bag, take a straight piece of rough ecru linen 48in. × 22in. (122cm × 56cm). Mark the position of the diamond eyelets and the area across each end which is to be smocked. There are eight rows of gathers ¾in. (2cm) apart, marked by counting the threads. Work the eyelets first in a soft thread in shades of a color, then gather the threads to fit the handle, and work Honeycomb smocking in a similar soft thread.

Work a row of Four-sided stitch down each long side of the fabric. Pleat the ends of the fabric, fold them over the bars of the handles and stitch them in place. Join the sides by whipping the two rows of stitching together. Cut a lining the width and twice the depth of the bag, fold in two and join the sides up to the point where they divide. Cut the upper part to fit the narrow part of the bag. Make a small hem and gather around the top opening of the wide part of the bag and pull it up tightly. Slip the lining into the bag and hem it in place.

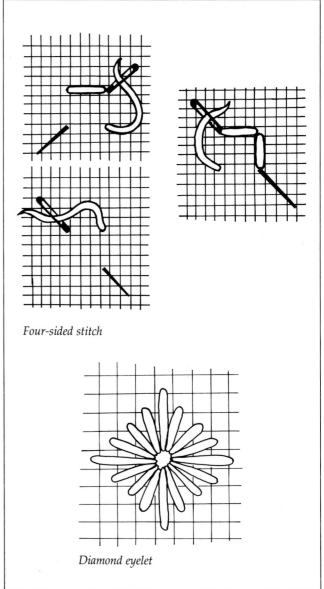

*Four-sided stitch*

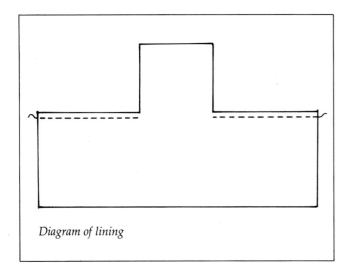

*Diagram of lining*

*Diamond eyelet*

110

**Workbag.** *By Margaret Darby. A heavy burlap has been embroidered with eyelets, and smocked onto a pair of wooden handles.*

This jacket is useful as a cover-up for a sun dress or T-shirt, or it could be used as a blouse.

Basically it is a raglan sleeved blouse with three-quarter sleeves, opening front, and straight hem with tiny slits at the seams.

The smocking is on the sleeves, which have a narrow hem turned over to the right side and edged with Holbein stitch in two colors. There are six rows of gathers, and the smocking is done in Diamond stitch, three rows parallel and three rows opposite.

**Cotton cheesecloth jacket.** *The front is embroidered and the sleeves are smocked in matching colors.*

The neck edge is turned under to enclose a drawstring, the hem line being covered with Holbein stitch in two colors, and beyond that a row of Herringbone stitch in one of the colors. The front is embroidered with Stem-stitch flowers radiating from a central eyelet, with leaves in Detached Chain. The front panel is edged with a row of Herringbone stitch enclosed in two rows of stem stitch.

# Smocking with patchwork

**Patchwork insert in smocked cushion.** *By Pat Roberts. A Somerset patchwork circle framed by a band of smocking, set in a plain cotton cover, in an interesting combination of techniques.*

# Gathering for surface texture

## NORTH AMERICAN SMOCKING

This is a form of smocking which gathers the surface of a fabric into folded patterns. It can be worked from the wrong or the right side of a fabric, and is often used for cushions where the pattern can be displayed to advantage.

The type of fabric you choose will contribute greatly to the finished effect. Satins and velvets will emphasize the richness of the surface, while matt linens and upholstery fabrics will yield patterns of greater softness and subtlety.

Use strong linen or cotton thread, or buttonhole twist. The dots can be marked on the front or the back as required, using a pencil and ruler; or you can make a template in thin cardboard pierced with holes and transfer the dots with pencil or chalk.

### Lattice pattern

This is worked on the wrong side of the fabric. The dots are about 1in. (25mm) apart and the rows about ½in. (12mm) apart.

Start at dot A and then make a small stitch over it (Fig. 1). Pick up dot B. Return to dot A and pick it up again. Pull A and B tightly together. Pick up dot C and, with the thread above the needle, slip it under the thread between AB and C and pull it tightly to make a knot, keeping the fabric flat between AB and C.

Pick up dot D, then pick up dot C and pull together tightly and make a knot. Pick up dot E, and with the thread above the needle slip it under the thread between D and E and make a knot. Repeat down the work for the required length. Work row 2 down the length. Repeat across the area.

### Flower pattern

This is worked on the right side of the fabric. The dots are about ½in. (12mm) apart in rows ½in. (12mm) apart.

Start at top left at 1A. Take a small diagonal stitch – and likewise at 2, 3 and 4 – all slanting towards the center of the square. Pull the thread very tightly and secure them all together with another small stitch. Take the needle to the wrong side, bring it out again at 1B and repeat. Work the necessary number of squares across the row. Work the required number of rows.

### Variant on flower pattern
*(see left cushion on page 115)*

This is worked on the wrong side of the fabric. The dots are ⅝in. (15mm) apart, placed in pairs 1¼in. (30mm) apart, and the rows are 1¼in. (30mm) apart.

Start at top left at 1A and take a small diagonal stitch. Then take a small diagonal stitch at 2, 3, and 4. All these slant towards the center of the square. Pull the thread very tightly, and then take another small diagonal stitch to secure the dots. Keeping the needle on the wrong side, start the next square at 1B. Work the rest of the squares across the row, then work the subsequent rows in the same way from left to right.

On the right side of the finished piece, push the folds through to the back, leaving the raised rolls of fabric at the corners of each square, as shown in the photograph.

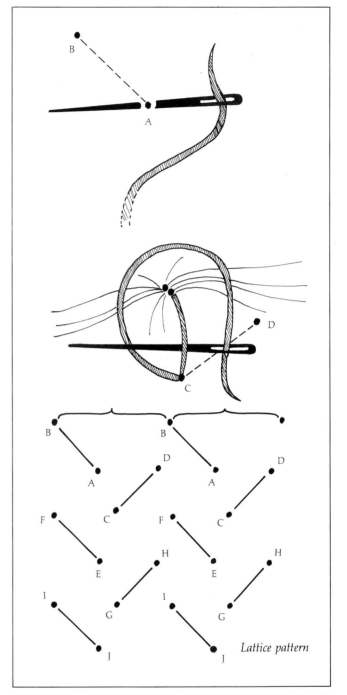

*Lattice pattern*

*Close-up of lattice pattern*

*Left.* **Smocked cushion.** *Lent by Jean Littlejohn. A regular pattern worked in reverse smocking, a variant of the Flower Pattern, as shown in the diagram.*

*Right.* **Smocked cushion.** *By Georgina Rees. A lozenge pattern worked in reverse smocking, as shown in the diagram, with a structure of Honeycomb stitches on the back of the gathers using a matching thread.*

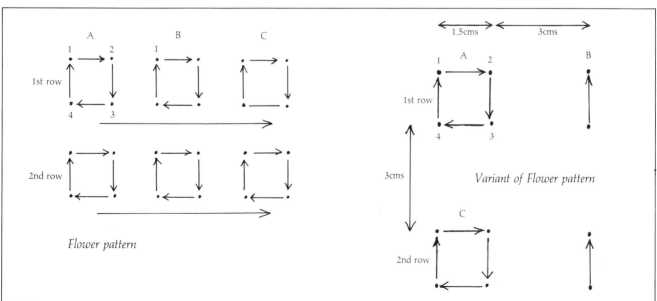

## Lozenge pattern

This is worked on the wrong side of the fabric, the dots being about ¾in. (20mm) apart and the rows being ⅜in. (10mm) apart.

In the first row join A to B with a small back stitch to catch the dots, and then down to join C to D similarly, and then up to join E to F, and so on.

In the second row join A to B as before, but then go up to join C to D and back down again to join E to F, and so on. Continue to work in rows until the space is filled.

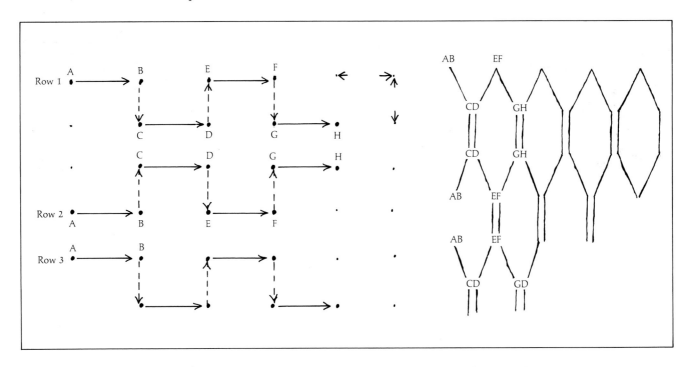

# CHAPTER 7

# Fastenings and finishes

*Bias strips – Rouleaux – Piping – Buttons
– Facings – Yokes – Stitches – Needle-
made edgings*

# Fastenings and finishes

## BIAS STRIPS

Bias strips can be cut from matching or contrasting fabric and used to bind necklines and cuffs, to make rouleaux, and to cover piping cord. They are cut on the bias so that the strips will stretch and can be applied to curves without wrinkling.

### Make bias strips as follows:

1. To find the true bias, pin out the fabric so that the grain is straight and cut to the thread. Fold over a raw edge and position it parallel with the selvage. The fold will be on the bias, that is to say, at a 45-degree angle to any straight edge.
2. From the back, mark down this first fold with a pencil and ruler; then mark the required width in lines parallel with the fold.
3. Cut along the marked lines. Join the lengths if required with a ¼in. (6mm) seam. Press the seam open and trim the edges.
4. As a sewing guide, fold the strip in half with the wrong sides together, and press. Turn under a small hem each side and press.

### To bind a straight edge

Lay the binding on the main fabric, right sides together, raw edges matching, and stitch along the seam line.

Turn the binding over to the wrong side, pin, and then slip-stitch the folded edge along the first line of stitching.

### To bind a curved edge

Fit the binding around the curve, and pin it in place with the pins at right angles to the seam line. Stitch along the seam line. Trim, layer and clip the raw edges. Turn binding over and slip-stitch to the wrong side.

### Slip stitch

Work from right to left. Bring out the needle through the folded hem of the binding. Make a tiny stitch by catching up a few threads from the main fabric, then re-insert the needle in the fold and run it along for ¼in. (6mm) before bringing it out and making another tiny stitch, again in the main fabric. This type of hem should be almost invisible.

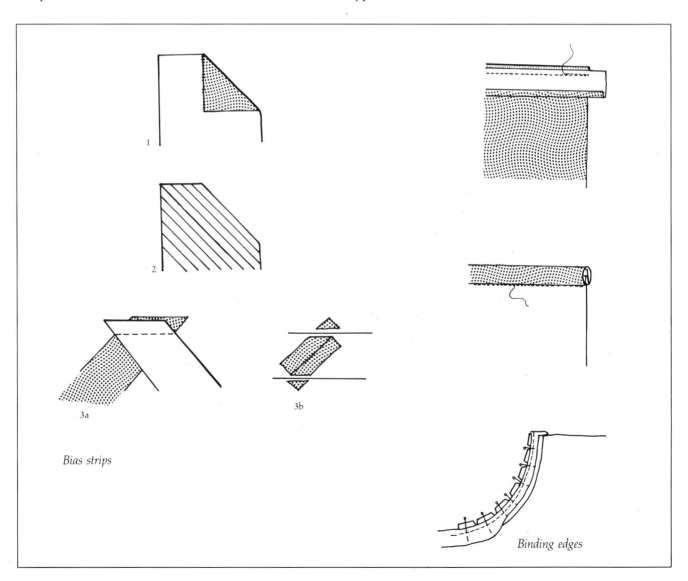

1

2

3a

3b

*Bias strips*

*Binding edges*

## ROULEAUX

A rouleau is a turned hollow tube made from a bias strip of fabric, which can be used for trimming or as a means of fastening either as a tie or a loop. It is often made of a contrasting fabric or color, and can also be made firmer by being filled with a narrow piping cord.

### Self-filled rouleau

Cut a number of bias strips about 1in.–1¼in. (2.8cm) wide. Join if required. Fold in half lengthwise, right sides together, and stitch along ¼in. (6mm) from the fold. Do not trim seam allowance. Using a blunt bodkin and some strong thread, fasten the thread at the seam at one end of the tubing and work the bodkin through the tube. Pull out the thread firmly, feeding the seam allowance into the other end of the tube until it is all turned through.

### Filled rouleau

Choose a suitable weight of narrow cord. Cut a number of bias strips of fabric the same width as the diameter of the cord plus 1in. (2.5cm). Cut twice the length of cord. Fold the fabric over half the cord, starting in the center, with right sides together. Secure the end of the cord and fabric, and stitch along the length close to the cord – a zipper foot is useful – stretching the bias strip slightly. Trim the seam allowances. Turn through by drawing the enclosed cord out of the tube – the free end will automatically feed in.

### To make a bound neckline with a rouleau tie

Cut bias strips to the required length. If there is a join, position this at the back of the neck. Starting from the center back, attach the binding to the outside of the neckline in the usual way. Stitch along the ends of the ties and turn them through. Roll over the neckline binding and slip-stitch to the wrong side.

### To make button loops

Make a length of rouleau and cut it into short lengths that fit the buttons. Position the loops as shown on the right side of the fabric. Lay the facing over the loops, right sides together. Stitch on seam line. Turn facing to the back, and press.

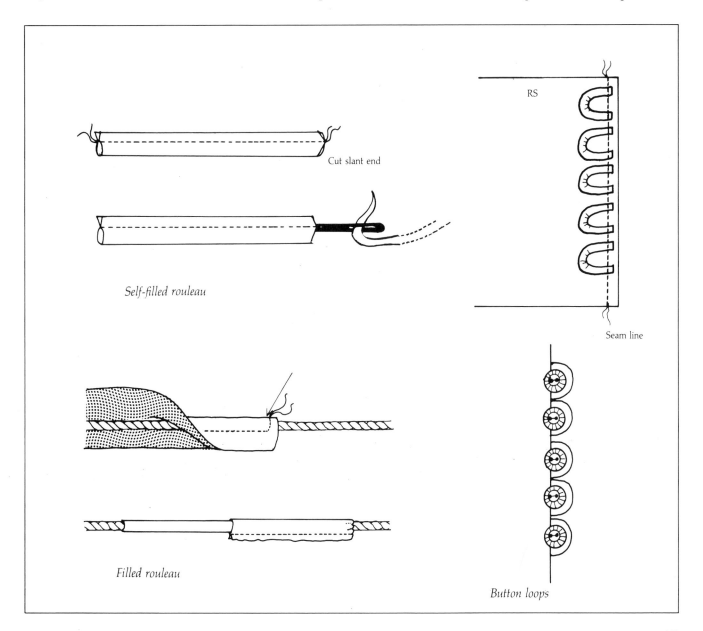

Cut slant end

*Self-filled rouleau*

RS

Seam line

*Filled rouleau*

*Button loops*

## Toggle fastening

For the loops, make the required number of rouleaux and fold in half. Stitch them together except for ½in. (12mm) at the loop end.

For each toggle, cut a 2in. (5cm) square of fabric. Turn under a ½in. (12mm) hem on three sides and press. With the raw edge inside, roll up into a toggle, stitching the long side and the ends. Insert into the rouleau loops and secure with a few stitches.

On the right side of the fabric, position the piping and rouleau loops. Cover with facing or binding, and stitch on the seam line close to the cord. Turn the facing to the back and stitch down. This fastening is shown on the vest on page 77.

## PIPING

Piping is made by covering a cord with a bias strip, the two flaps being inserted in a seam. The bias strips should be cut with sufficient width to give a seam allowance similar to that of the main fabric.

Piping cord is available in different sizes; the type and weight should be chosen to suit the fabric. If the piping cord has not been pre-shrunk, it should be boiled for three minutes and dried thoroughly before use.

### To make piping

Make a bias strip of the required length. Lay the cord down the center of the wrong side of the strip, fold the fabric over and pin and baste beside the cord, wrong sides together. Stitch down close to the cord, using a zipper foot.

### To join piping

Try not to make a join at corners or in a prominent place.

Join the piping before inserting it in the seam. Where the ends of the cord meet, unravel about 1in. (2.5cm) at each end, trim the strands to different lengths and twist them around each other before stitching up the fabric.

### Piping over smocking

Make the required length of piping. On the right side, pin and baste the piping along the top gathering row. Although it is not shown in the diagram this edge will have to be neatened with a yoke, binding, facing or lining, so lay this over the piping and the smocking, right sides together. Stitch through all layers close to the cord. Press into place.

## TO MAKE A PIPED CUSHION COVER

When the smocked side is completed, pin it out, measure it, and mark the size on the wrong side. Cut out the plain side to match, with seam allowance all round. Decide on type of closing. If a zipper is needed, insert this in the plain side first.

Measure the circumference of the cushion – it is easier to put in piping if the corners are rounded. Make the required length of piping, and join the ends. Make sure the join does not come at a corner. Pin, baste and stitch the piping to the right side of the smocked piece, notching the seam allowance on the corners. Lay the plain side face down over it, pin, baste and stitch round through all layers as close as possible to the piping cord. Trim and layer the seams. Turn through.

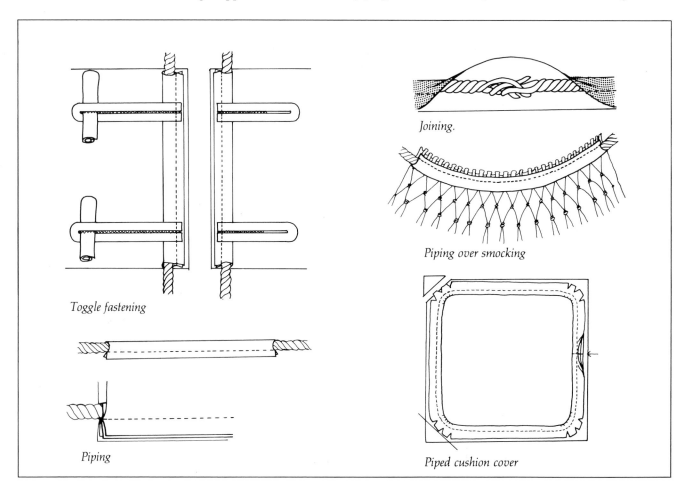

Toggle fastening

Piping

Joining.

Piping over smocking

Piped cushion cover

## BUTTONS

Hand-made buttons go particularly well with smocking. They can be made in shaded silks or wools, or matching or contrasting fabric, and can be combined with beads with decorative effect, as in the Birdseye pattern.

### Dorset buttons

The traditional fastening for many smocks was the hand-made Dorset button. This was constructed by embroidery over small rings and their manufacture once formed a flourishing local industry. The types illustrated here are the Crosswheel and the Birdseye.

The various stages of making the Dorset button have traditional names, and they are all worked on rings. These can be made of metal or bone, and come in various sizes to suit the garment.

Use wool, linen, cotton or silk thread, and be sure it is long enough as threads cannot be joined easily – allow at least 2¾ yards (2½ meters). Use a blunt-ended tapestry needle for the embroidery, and a pointed one for finishing off.

Keep the buttonhole stitches firm and close, and make sure the ring is covered. To begin, tie the yarn to the ring and hold the loose end while you work the first few stitches over it, then cut off the excess.

### The Crosswheel button

**Casting.** Cover the ring with buttonhole stitches. When you get back to the beginning, slip the needle through the first stitch again so that the join does not show.

**Slicking.** Turn the stitches inward so that the outside is smooth and the ridge is on the inside.

**Laying.** Bring the thread from the back at the bottom of the ring and up and over the center. Continue to wind round making a number of spokes, and then secure the center with cross-stitches, pulling it into position.

**Rounding.** Starting from the center, work back-stitch round the spokes – first under 1 and 2, then under 2 and 3. When the button is filled, make a few stitches in the center at the back to secure the thread, then leave the thread for fastening to the garment.

### The Birdseye button

This is a very small button made on a ring about ½in. (12mm) across. After casting and slicking, a small bead is sewn into the center of the ring, filling it up.

### Fabric-covered buttons

Button molds can be purchased, over which fabric is laid and clipped into position.

Embroidery of various kinds can be worked on the fabric covering the button molds. Cut out circles of fabric, and then try one on the mold and mark round the circumference of the visible circle. Work the embroidery in the center, and then assemble the button as instructed.

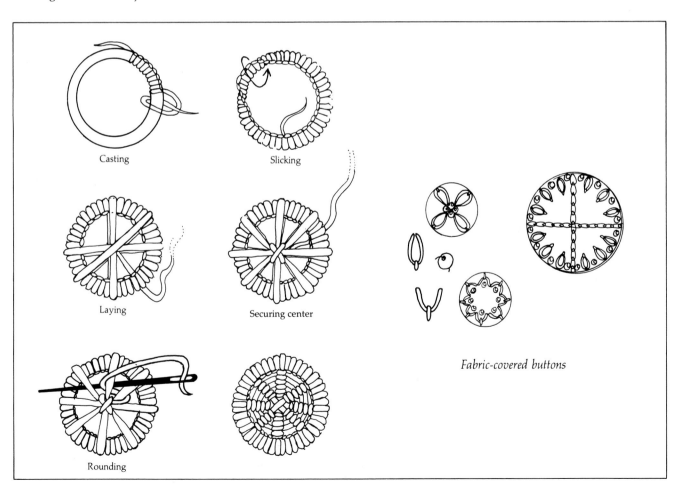

Casting

Slicking

Laying

Securing center

Rounding

*Fabric-covered buttons*

## FACINGS
### Second line of stitching

Neck, cuff, and openings all require facings, and these are generally worked in the usual way. However, where the fabric is silk or of a springy texture, a final row of stitching on the right side makes a better and crisper finish. It adds strength, and obviates the need for hard pressing, leaving a softer finish on a fine silk. It also keeps the facing to the inside of the garment.

### Method

1. Cut a facing and interfacing, the same grain and shape as the edge.
2. Apply the facing in the usual way, right sides together, matching any seams or balance marks. Baste and stitch.
3. Trim the seam allowance to different levels, making the interfacing (if used) the shortest and the garment layer the longest.
4. Snip the seam allowance on a curved edge.
5. Lightly press facing and turnings in same direction and away from the garment.
6. Work a line of machine stitching on the right side following the seam line through both facings and turnings.

## YOKES

### Triple layer for soft fabric

Where smocking has to be set into a yoke of soft thin fabric, a better appearance will be achieved if you use a third layer of fabric. This could be the same as the garment, or an interlining or cotton fabric. The thickness will then hold the smocking more securely, and will also conceal the seam allowances.

### Method

1. Cut yoke and yoke lining, plus one extra layer.
2. Lay yoke and extra layer together and baste on seam line.
3. Set the smocking onto this double yoke.
4. Use yoke lining to neaten the inside. Make the shoulder seams first and then set it on as a facing at the neck edge.
5. On the wrong side, pull the yoke lining down, turn under seam allowance and pin and sew into place over the smocking gathers.

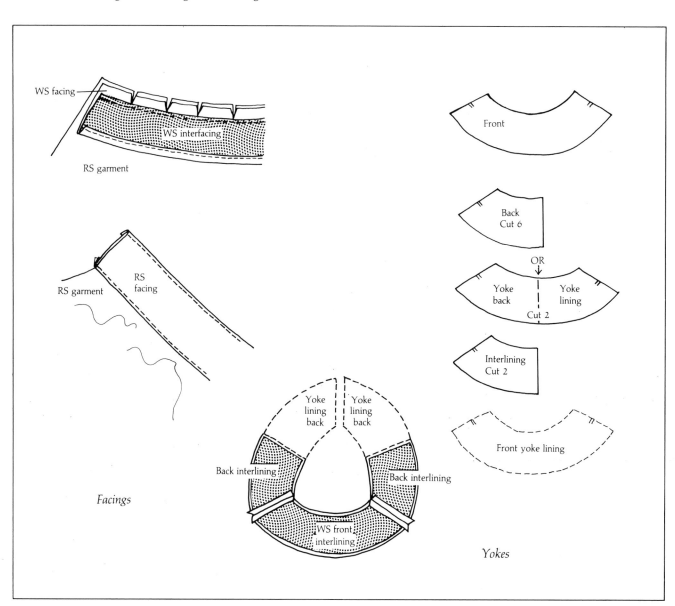

*Facings*

*Yokes*

## STITCHES

### Bullion knot

Bullion knots take a little practice to make. They also need a firm rounded thread and a thick needle with a narrow eye.

Bring the thread through at the arrow. Insert the needle further back to the right, the length of the required stitch, and bring it out at the arrow again. Do not pull through, but twist the thread around it about six times – enough to fill the stitch – and then press the roll back towards the fabric with the left thumb and pull the needle carefully through both the fabric and the twists. Lift the needle and thread back towards the beginning of the stitch to persuade the little roll of thread to lie in the proper position, tighten up and then insert the needle into the same hole and take it through to the back.

### Eyelets

Use fabric where the threads can be counted. The stitches are all taken into the same central hole. The one shown is worked over a square of eight threads.

### Feather stitch

Work this from the top downwards, making looped stitches on alternate sides of the line. If worked with two stitches to the left and then two to the right, the stitch becomes Double Feather stitch.

### French knot

Bring the thread through where the knot is to lie. Wrap the thread several times around the needle, using the thumb and first finger of the other hand to hold the thread taut. Still keeping the thread taut, swing the needle round and go down through the fabric close to the entry point, pulling the needle and thread smoothly through the twists. If the knots are being worked on a line, the needle emerges again at the required spot and the pulling through is done in one movement. However, if the fabric is on a frame it is more satisfactory to work the knot in two movements. It should lie on the surface like a bead. If the knot is too small, try using a thicker thread.

### Herringbone stitch

This is usually worked from left to right. Insert the needle horizontally, pointing to the left, and take a stitch at the top and bottom of the line alternately. Different effects can be made by varying the size of the stitches and the space between them.

### Stem stitch

Work from bottom to top. Bring up the needle at the beginning of the line and take a little stitch further along, going in slightly to the right of the line and coming out slightly to the left of it. Continue in this way, making a long stitch forward and a short stitch back. The greater the angle to the line of work, the wider the finished line.

### Woven wheel

A simple woven wheel consists of an uneven number of threads thrown over a circle, which are then woven around with another thread laced over and under these spokes. Use a blunt tapestry needle. A ribbed wheel has an even number of foundation threads, which are covered with a continuous line of back stitch worked from the center outwards.

### Slip stitch

A dressmaking stitch used to catch down a hem. Come up through the main fabric, insert the needle in the hem, and slip it along the fold for a short way. Bring it out, and then take up a few threads of the main fabric. In this way a line of stitching can be almost invisible.

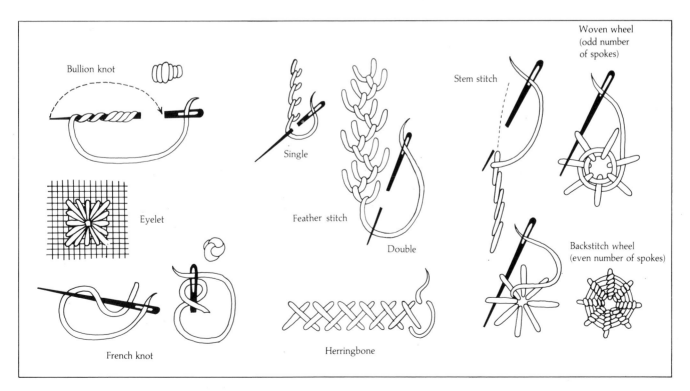

Bullion knot

Eyelet

French knot

Single

Feather stitch

Double

Herringbone

Stem stitch

Woven wheel (odd number of spokes)

Backstitch wheel (even number of spokes)

*Every kind of smocking*

### Needle-made edgings

These delicate little edgings make an attractive finish to cuffs, collars or bodices, especially if worked in colors which pick up those in the smocking.

The edge to be decorated should be a finished hem, to make a strong base for the stitches.

Use a firm round thread for best effect – coton à broder or a fine crochet cotton.

### Antwerp edging stitch

This is a knotted Buttonhole stitch used as an edging, which can be a single or a double row.

Bring the needle out through the hem and work evenly spaced knotted Buttonhole stitches, each stitch going through both layers of fabric on the edge of the hem. The second row is worked into the first, the knots lying between those in the first row.

### Armenian edging stitch

This gives a scroll-like finish if a firm thread is used. Bring the needle out through the hem, and insert it from behind a little way along. Pull the thread through part of the way, leaving a small loop. Twist the loop with the other hand, crossing the thread as shown, and slip the needle through the loop. Pull the thread through while still holding the loop, then tighten the knot against the edge before making the next stitch. Work evenly spaced knots right along the hem.

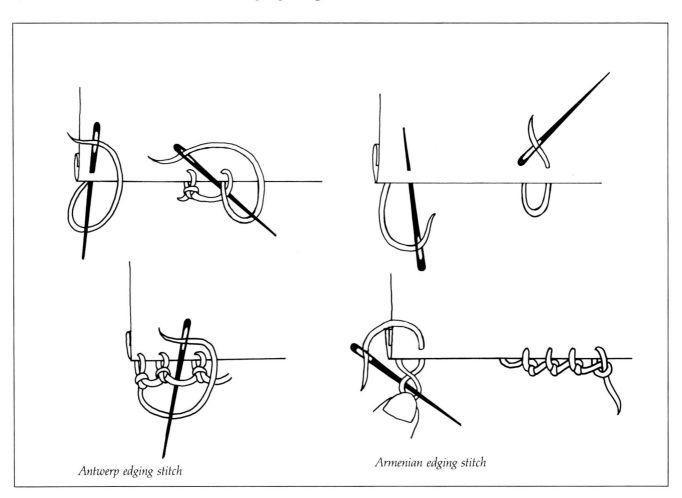

*Antwerp edging stitch*

*Armenian edging stitch*

**Braid edging stitch**

Bring the needle out through the hem, wrap the thread clockwise around the thumb, then slip the needle upwards through the loop and behind the fold to emerge through the double layers pointing upwards. Loop the thread round the needle, thus tightening the lower loop, and pull the thread through holding the needle first up, and then down, to secure the knot. Work evenly spaced stitches along the hem. The loops thus formed can be buttonholed over, as in the next stitch described, or another row of Braid edging stitch can be worked between the knots of the first row.

**Buttonholed edge**

Work a row of spaced Buttonhole stitch along the hem, and then work another row filling in the loops with close Buttonhole.

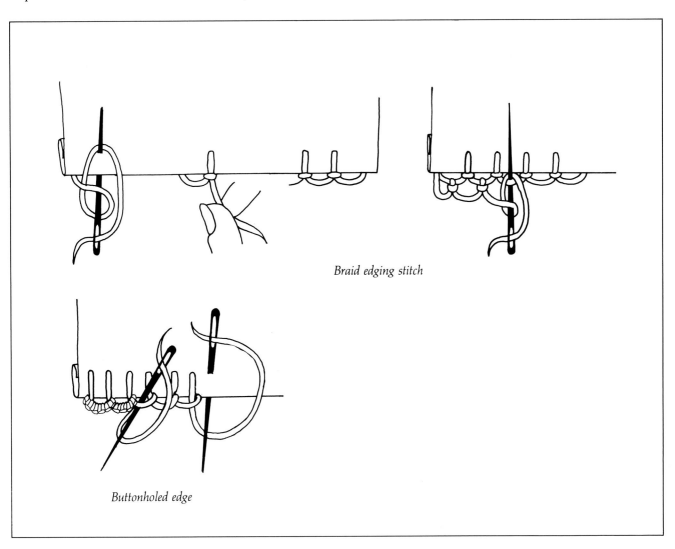

*Braid edging stitch*

*Buttonholed edge*

**Useful Addresses**
The Smocking Group
The Embroiderers' Guild
Apartment 41A
Hampton Court Palace
East Molesey
Surrey, England

The Smocking Arts Guild of America
PO Box 75
Knoxville
TN 37901, USA

**List of contributors**
Sue Atkinson
Margaret Blow
Olive Camplin
Mary Cornall
Isabella Crocker
Margaret Darby
Diana Keay
Jean Littlejohn
Sheila Markham
Gail Marsh
Rachel Newall
Bryony Nielsen
Georgina Rees
Chris Reid
Dorothy Reglar
Pat Roberts
Sheila Shaw
Pat Steward
Sheila Sturrock
Ann Tranquillini
May Williams
Marie Zambra

# INDEX